01/12

# celebrating
# PARTY FOODS

Mini Lemon Cupcakes, Lemon-Rosemary Pecans, and
Raspberry-Lemon Punch, recipes on pages 14-15

LEISURE ARTS, INC.
Little Rock, Arkansas

**EDITORIAL STAFF**

**Editor in Chief:** Susan White Sullivan
**Craft Publications Director:** Cheryl Johnson
**Special Projects Director:** Susan Frantz Wiles
**Foods Editor:** Jane Kenner Prather
**Contributing Foods Editor:** Celia Fahr Harkey, R.D.
**Editorial Writer:** Merrilee Gasaway
**Contributing Test Kitchen Assistants:** Nora Faye
    Spencer Clift, Marcelle Castleberry, and
    Rose Glass Klein
**Senior Prepress Director:** Mark Hawkins
**Art Publications Director:** Rhonda Shelby
**Art Category Manager:** Lora Puls
**Senior Publications Designer:** Dana Vaughn
**Imaging Technician:** Stephanie Johnson
**Photography Manager:** Katherine Laughlin
**Contributing Photographer:** Mark Mathews
**Contributing Photo Stylist:** Christy Myers
**Publishing Systems Administrator:** Becky Riddle
**Mac Information Technology Specialist:**
    Robert Young

**BUSINESS STAFF**

**President and Chief Executive Officer:**
    Rick Barton
**Vice President and Chief Operations Officer:**
    Tom Siebenmorgen
**Vice President of Sales:**
    Mike Behar
**Director of Finance and Administration:**
    Laticia Mull Dittrich
**National Sales Director:** Martha Adams
**Creative Services Director:** Chaska Lucas
**Information Technology Director:** Hermine Linz
**Controller:** Francis Caple
**Vice President, Operations:** Jim Dittrich
**Retail Customer Service Manager:** Stan Raynor
**Print Production Manager:** Fred F. Pruss

Library of Congress Control Number: 2011930139
ISBN-13: 978-1-60900-308-1

# contents

Tunnel Cake (from left),
Chocolate Shortbread, and
Chewy Chocolate Bars, recipes
on pages 127-128

Alfredo Mushroom Sauce
on spinach fettucine (front,
right); Marinara Sauce on
bow tie pasta (left); and
Spinach Pasta Sauce on
tortellini, with Sparkling
Lime Spritzer, recipes on
pages 34-35

# celebrating
# PARTY FOODS

Hosting parties for lots of different occasions will be a
breeze for even the novice cook with this collection of
menus and party food recipes. Thirteen themes and
101 recipes are featured, offering entertainment for all
age groups. Parties range from an elegant bridal shower
and chocolate indulgence to a casual meal for sports fans
and a pasta party for girls' night out. Some plans call for
a variety of snacks and sweets, while others feature a
complete dinner. Each party theme provides a starter menu
with kitchen-tested recipes plus ideas to enhance the fun.
General cooking tips are included, along with expert advice
for Success with Parties. Let's celebrate!

Lemon Cream Stuffed Grapes,
recipe on page 16

# SUCCESS WITH PARTIES

You can be most successful at hosting parties when you know a few tips from the pros. Here are some of our favorites.

## PLANNING TIPS

- Good food is the key to making everyone happy. Plan your menu thoughtfully.
- Read and study your chosen recipes carefully in advance. Preparations will go much smoother if you know what to expect once you start cooking.
- Consider trying out the recipes ahead of time; you'll learn whether you want to make any adjustments in the seasonings, and your family will enjoy the treat!
- Arrange to borrow or rent extra dinnerware, trays, table linens, chairs, etc.

## HOSTESS TIPS

- Remember what's important is that your guests feel comfortable and have a good time. Relax—and let your cheerful mood set the tone for everyone else.
- Practice makes perfect! The more experience you get in hosting parties, the more confident you will feel.

## FOOD PREPARATION TIPS

- For convenience and efficiency, organize all your ingredients and tools before you start mixing or cooking. Pre-measure ingredients in individual bowls, cups, or bags and set aside until needed.
- Take advantage of opportunities to do some of the work ahead of time. Is there a recipe that can be prepared (fully or partially) and stored in the refrigerator or freezer until needed?
- If it won't compromise quality in a particular instance, substitute frozen fruit or other ingredients.

- Consider supplementing your menu with convenience items: meats from the deli or a barbecue restaurant, popular side dishes from local cafeterias, cakes and rolls from the bakery, etc.

## COOKING AND BAKING TIPS

- Use heavy-gauge pans for even heating. For breads, use shiny aluminum pans. Dark coating on pans will affect browning. Many cooks prefer clear glass bakeware for pies and other pastry because of how efficiently glass conducts heat and because you can see when the bottom crust is sufficiently browned.
- Preheat your oven long enough for it to reach the correct temperature given in the recipe.
- Bake one loaf or pan of the recipe at a time on the center rack of a preheated oven. If baking two loaves or pans at a time, space evenly for good air circulation.
- Oven temperatures vary, so always check your food 1 minute before the earliest time stated in recipe, to prevent overbaking.
- When you need to drizzle a small amount of icing or topping and you do not have a pastry bag, use a resealable plastic bag. After filling bag half full of icing or topping, seal the bag and cut off a small tip of one corner. Make your first snip small, as you can always cut off more if needed.

NOTE: For more advice, see Kitchen Tips on page 138.

# CHILD'S BIRTHDAY

Get ready for big smiles and lots of giggles at this fun birthday celebration for kids! Cute cupcakes and colorful snack mix will grab their attention and replenish their energy in between party games and activities. Moms will love the easy preparations needed for these simple recipes.

## recipes

**Ice-Cream Cone Cupcakes**
**Munch Mix**
**Chocolate Yogurt Shakes**

**Shown on opposite page:** Double the fun with cupcakes that look like ice-cream cones, served with frosty-cold Chocolate Yogurt Shakes. Colorful Munch Mix full of bite-size candies and snacks will help entertain hungry kids until it's time for the cupcakes

## party tips

• Cupcakes are perfect for children's parties. Besides being so cute, they are just the right serving size for kids. Also, cupcakes are much easier to serve than cutting and dishing out cake slices.

• There are lots of fun ways to display cupcakes. Cupcake tiers are especially handy, as are tiered cake stands. Use your imagination! We filled a deep dish with mini pretzels to keep our ice-cream cone cupcakes standing and to provide extra snacks afterward!

• If you still want the tradition of a big cake with candles to blow out, mass the cupcakes together. After the birthday boy or girl has made a wish, remove the candles and pass out the cupcakes, starting with those on the outer edge.

• Make snack foods available as soon as guests arrive, so that hungry kids will be less likely to sample the cupcakes too early. After all, you don't want that smiley face cupcake to lose its jelly bean nose!

• Use your scrapbooking supplies to make personalized tags for little party favor buckets of snack mix (see page 10).

# ice-cream cone cupcakes

For cupcakes, follow cake mix directions to combine cake mix, water, oil, and eggs. Fill each ice-cream cone with about 2½ tablespoons of batter. Place cones in cups of a muffin pan to keep cones upright. Bake in a preheated 350° oven for 20 to 25 minutes or until a toothpick inserted in center of cupcake comes out clean. Cool completely.

For icing, beat all ingredients together in a large bowl until smooth. Mound icing atop each cupcake to resemble ice cream. Before icing hardens, decorate with sprinkles, colored sugars, and candies.

To serve, nestle cupcakes into a dish of miniature pretzels or other snack mix.

**YIELD:** 30

**CUPCAKES**

- 1 package (18.25 ounces) chocolate cake mix
- 1¼ cups water
- ½ cup vegetable oil
- 3 eggs
- 30 small flat-bottomed ice-cream cones

**ICING**

- 5 cups confectioners sugar
- ¾ cup vegetable shortening
- ½ cup butter or margarine, softened
- 2½ tablespoons milk
- 1¼ teaspoons almond extract
    Assorted purchased sprinkles, colored sugars, and candies to decorate
    Fish-shaped pretzel crackers to serve

# munch mix

Create a special treat by mixing together colorful candies with miniature marshmallows, cookies, and crackers. The kids will have fun picking their favorite tastes and textures out of the jumble.

# chocolate yogurt shakes

In a blender, combine all ingredients; process until well blended. Serve immediately.

**YIELD:** about eight 6-ounce servings

- 2 cups chocolate milk
- 2 cups chocolate frozen yogurt, softened
- 2 cups crushed ice
- ½ cup chocolate syrup

# BABY SHOWER

When Baby's almost here, sweeten the growing excitement with a shower of gifts to help the mom-to-be prepare. As friends and family arrive, direct them to the food table to get snacks and punch to enjoy while mingling. Tiny decorated cupcakes are an easy-to-serve substitute for the traditional cake, and toasted nuts are always welcomed for counterbalancing the sweetness of the main offerings. Cookies and grapes are the ultimate choice for nibbling, and a creamy punch is extra refreshing.

## recipes

**Raspberry-Lemon Punch**
**Mini Lemon Cupcakes**
**Lemon-Rosemary Pecans**
**Lemon Cream Stuffed Grapes**
**Lemon-Ginger Cookies**

**Shown on opposite page:**
Raspberry-Lemon Punch is a refreshing blend of pink lemonade, raspberry sherbet, and lemon-lime soda. Adorable Mini Lemon Cupcakes are easy to decorate with pastel sprinkles. Lemon-Rosemary Pecans complement the sweet flavors.

## party tips

• With colorful food and sweetly wrapped packages serving as the center of attention, there's no need for an elaborate centerpiece. Just drape a pretty cloth (or maybe even receiving blankets!) on the table and arrange coordinating napkins and snack ware.

• For entertainment, plan a couple of easy games, such as baby bingo, word scramble, and "guess how many diaper pins are in the bottle." The ideas are endless when you search online for "baby shower games."

• Ask guests to bring index cards bearing their favorite child-care advice. Assemble these in a pocket photo album for the expectant mom to take home.

• When it's time to open the gifts, have scissors and a trash bag handy. To make things easier later on the new mom, have someone make a list of the gifts as they are opened. Pass out envelopes for the gift-givers to self-address, for thank-you cards to be sent.

Raspberry-Lemon Punch

Mini Lemon Cupcakes

Lemon-Rosemary Pecans

# raspberry-lemon punch

*Prepare ice ring a day ahead of time.*

For ice ring, combine 1 can pink lemonade concentrate and 3 cups water in a half-gallon container. Pour $3^1/_2$ cups lemonade in an 8-cup ring mold; reserve remaining lemonade. Freeze ice ring 4 hours.

Place lemon slices about 1 inch apart over frozen lemonade. Place raspberries between slices. Pour remaining 1 cup lemonade over fruit. Cover and freeze until firm.

To serve, combine remaining can lemonade concentrate and remaining 3 cups water in a half-gallon container. Pour lemonade into a punch bowl; add spoonfuls of sherbet. Add lemon-lime soda; stir until blended. Dip ice mold into warm water 15 seconds. Place ice ring in punch bowl. Serve immediately.

**YIELD:** about $5^1/_4$ quarts

2 cans (12 ounces each) pink lemonade concentrate, thawed and divided

6 cups water, divided

1 lemon, thinly sliced

6 whole fresh or frozen raspberries

1 half-gallon raspberry sherbet

4 cans (12 ounces each) lemon-lime soda, chilled

# mini lemon cupcakes

Line miniature muffin pans with paper baking cups; set aside.

Cream butter, shortening, and sugar in a large bowl until fluffy. In a small bowl, combine cake flour, baking powder, and salt. In another small bowl, combine milk and lemon extract. Alternately add dry ingredients and milk mixture to creamed mixture. In a small bowl, beat egg whites until stiff; fold into creamed mixture. Spoon batter into prepared pans, filling each cup three-fourths full.

Bake in a preheated 350° oven for 12 to 15 minutes or until a toothpick inserted in center of cupcake comes out clean. Remove from pans and cool on a wire rack.

Spoon frosting into a pastry bag fitted with a medium round tip. Pipe frosting on top of each cupcake; decorate with sprinkles.

**YIELD:** about $4^1/_2$ dozen

$1/_2$ cup butter or margarine, softened

$1/_4$ cup vegetable shortening

$1^1/_4$ cups sugar

$1^3/_4$ cups sifted cake flour

$1/_2$ teaspoon baking powder

$1/_8$ teaspoon salt

$2/_3$ cup milk

1 teaspoon lemon extract

3 egg whites

1 can (16 ounces) creamy vanilla frosting

Pastel sprinkles

# lemon-rosemary pecans

Place pecans in a medium bowl. In a small microwave-safe bowl, combine butter, rosemary, lemon zest, Worcestershire sauce, lemon pepper, and salt; microwave until butter melts. Pour over pecans; stir until well coated. Spread pecans, in a single layer, on an ungreased jellyroll pan. Bake at 250° for 45 minutes or until pecans are toasted, stirring every 15 minutes. Cool on pan.

**YIELD:** about 4 cups

4 cups pecan halves

$1/_3$ cup butter

3 to 4 tablespoons finely chopped fresh rosemary

2 teaspoons grated lemon zest

1 teaspoon Worcestershire sauce

1 teaspoon lemon pepper

$1/_2$ teaspoon salt

A cinnamon-spice blend enhances the delicate flavor of dried lemon peel and ground ginger in these sugar-coated Lemon-Ginger Cookies. Lemon Cream Stuffed Grapes are delightful morsels that will bring guests back to the table for more.

# lemon cream stuffed grapes

*Grapes may be prepared and refrigerated up to 4 hours before serving.*

In a medium bowl, beat cream cheese, confectioners sugar, lemon juice, and lemon zest until smooth. Spoon cream cheese mixture into a pastry bag fitted with a medium star tip. Cover tip and chill 2 hours.

Use a sharp knife to cut an "X" through top of each grape, being careful not to cut through bottom. Spread sections apart slightly. Pipe mixture into each grape. Garnish, if desired.

**YIELD:** about 3$^1$/$_2$ dozen

1 package (8 ounces) cream cheese, softened
$^1$/$_3$ cup confectioners sugar
1 tablespoon freshly squeezed lemon juice
1 teaspoon freshly grated lemon zest
1 pound large red and green seedless grapes
**GARNISH:** lemon zest strips

# lemon-ginger cookies

In a large bowl, combine flour, ginger, lemon peel, baking soda, salt, cinnamon, cloves, and nutmeg. In another large bowl, cream butter and brown sugar until fluffy. Add molasses and egg; beat until smooth. Add dry ingredients; stir until a soft dough forms. Shape dough into 1-inch balls; roll each ball in sugar. Place on a greased baking sheet. Bake in a preheated 350° oven for 8 to 10 minutes or until lightly browned on bottom. Place on a wire rack to cool.

**YIELD:** about 7 dozen

2$^1$/$_2$ cups all-purpose flour
1 tablespoon ground ginger
2 teaspoons dried lemon peel
2 teaspoons baking soda
$^1$/$_2$ teaspoon salt
$^1$/$_2$ teaspoon ground cinnamon
$^1$/$_4$ teaspoon ground cloves
$^1$/$_4$ teaspoon ground nutmeg
$^3$/$_4$ cup butter or margarine, softened
1 cup firmly packed brown sugar
$^1$/$_4$ cup molasses
1 egg
Granulated sugar

# BRIDAL SHOWER

Elegant finger foods and champagne punch are fitting fare for a party where friends and family shower a bride-to-be with gifts to furnish her new home. Start off light with *crudités* and flaky pockets of cheese topped with tangy sauce. Then invite everyone to reward themselves with tantalizing tidbits of cheesecake and candied walnuts. The sophisticated refreshments set a refined mood for a party linked to such a momentous milestone.

## recipes

**Cranberry-Brie in Pastry**
**Champagne Punch**
**Light Cucumber-Dill Dip**
**Toffee Walnuts**
**Mint Cheesecake Bites**

**Shown on opposite page:**
Flavorful but light selections for a bridal shower include petite Cranberry-Brie in Pastry and an assortment of fresh vegetables to serve with Light Cucumber-Dill Dip. The zingy Champagne Punch combines fruit juices, brandy, and chilled bubbly.

## party tips

• You can't go wrong using flowers to decorate at wedding showers, whether it's fresh blossoms on the table or a floral cloth underneath it all.

• Coordinate your party décor with the couple's wedding colors. Afterward, let some of the decorations, such as the table cloth, vase, or platter, be gifts for the bride's new home.

• The Internet has a vast supply of entertainment ideas; search for ice-breaker activities and party games such as dating trivia, complete the sentence, groom's interview, and more.

• When it's time to open the gifts, have a trash bag handy but hide the scissors—remind the bride about the old wives' tale that every ribbon she cuts represents how many babies the couple will have! Then watch how inventive she can be at opening those packages!

• Ask someone to make a list of the gifts as they are opened, in case items get separated from their package tags.

• Supply a set of thank-you cards and pass out the envelopes for gift-givers to self-address. These envelopes can also be placed in a bowl or bag and used for drawing names of door prize winners.

Champagne Punch

Cranberry-Brie in Pastry

Light Cucumber-Dill Dip

# cranberry-brie in pastry

In a small saucepan, heat oil over medium heat. Add onion and celery; cook until tender. Stir in cranberry sauce, sour cream, and vinegar. Stirring occasionally, bring to a boil over medium heat and cook 15 minutes or until thickened. Remove from heat; set aside.

Spray each sheet of phyllo pastry with cooking spray. Stack pastry sheets on top of each other; cut into eighteen 3-inch squares. Press pastry squares into each cup of a greased miniature muffin pan. Place 1 piece of cheese in center of pastry square. Spoon a heaping teaspoonful of cranberry mixture over top of cheese. Bake in a preheated 375° oven for 12 to 15 minutes or until golden brown. Serve warm.

YIELD: 1½ dozen

2   teaspoons vegetable oil
¼   cup finely chopped onion
¼   cup finely chopped celery
1   can (16 ounces) whole berry cranberry sauce
2   tablespoons sour cream
1   teaspoon balsamic vinegar
4   sheets frozen phyllo pastry, thawed according to package directions
    Vegetable cooking spray
1   package (4½ ounces) Brie cheese, cut into 18 small pieces

# champagne punch

Combine cranberry juice, pineapple juice, and brandy in a large punch bowl. Stir in champagne; serve immediately.

**YIELD:** about 18 cups

1 bottle (64 ounces) cranberry juice cocktail, chilled

1 can (12 ounces) frozen pineapple juice concentrate, thawed

2 cups brandy

2 bottles (750 ml each) champagne, chilled

# light cucumber-dill dip

*This is a great low-calorie dip with only 7 calories per tablespoon!*

Process cream cheese, cottage cheese, green onion, lemon juice, salt, dill weed, and black pepper in a food processor until smooth. Add cucumber; pulse process just until blended. Cover and chill 2 hours to allow flavors to blend.

Garnish, if desired. Serve with fresh vegetables.

**YIELD:** about 2 cups

4 ounces fat-free cream cheese

$1/2$ cup fat-free cottage cheese

1 tablespoon chopped green onion

2 teaspoons freshly squeezed lemon juice

$3/4$ teaspoon salt

$1/2$ teaspoon chopped fresh dill weed

$1/8$ teaspoon pepper

1 cucumber peeled, seeded, and coarsely chopped

GARNISH: chopped green onion tops

Fresh vegetables to serve

Mint Cheesecake Bites are an easy way to offer dessert when calorie-smart guests are likely to say, "Just a tiny piece for me, please." Pretty condiment cups lend pizzazz to single servings of Toffee Walnuts.

# toffee walnuts

Bake walnuts on a baking sheet at 350° for about 8 minutes or until lightly toasted, stirring after 4 minutes. Turn off oven. Cover toasted walnuts with aluminum foil on baking sheet. Return to oven to stay warm.

Line another baking sheet with aluminum foil; grease foil. Set aside.

Butter sides of a very heavy large saucepan. Combine butter, sugar, water, corn syrup, and salt in saucepan. Stirring constantly, cook over medium-low heat until sugar dissolves. Using a pastry brush dipped in hot water, wash down any sugar crystals on sides of pan. Attach a candy thermometer to pan, making sure thermometer does not touch bottom of pan. Increase heat to medium and bring to a boil. Cook, without stirring, until mixture reaches hard-crack stage (approximately 300° to 310°). Test about ¹/₂ teaspoon mixture in ice water. Mixture will form brittle threads in ice water and will remain brittle when removed from water. Remove from heat and stir in warm walnuts and vanilla. Spread mixture onto prepared baking sheet; sprinkle with salt. Using 2 forks, pull walnuts apart on baking sheet. Let walnuts cool.

**YIELD:** about 7¹/₂ cups

- 1 pound walnut halves (about 4¹/₂ cups)
- 1 cup butter
- 1 cup sugar
- ¹/₃ cup water
- 1 tablespoon light corn syrup
- ¹/₄ teaspoon salt
- 1 teaspoon vanilla extract
- Salt

# mint cheesecake bites

Combine cookie crumbs and butter; press mixture into an aluminum foil-lined 9 x 13-inch baking pan. Bake at 350° for 10 minutes. Cool on a wire rack.

Beat cream cheese and sugar at medium speed of an electric mixer until creamy. Add eggs, one at a time, beating just until blended after each addition. Stir in peppermint extract and food coloring. Spread cream cheese mixture over prepared crust. Bake at 300° for 35 minutes or until set. Cool on a wire rack. Cover and chill 8 hours.

Cut into 1 x 2-inch bars. Cut each candy in half diagonally; place on each piece. Store in refrigerator.

**YIELD:** 4 dozen

- 3 cups chocolate sandwich cookie crumbs (40 cookies)
- ¹/₂ cup butter or margarine, melted
- 4 packages (8 ounces each) cream cheese, softened
- 1 cup sugar
- 4 large eggs
- 1¹/₂ teaspoons peppermint extract
- 6 drops green liquid food coloring
- 24 chocolate-mint layered candies

# BOOK CLUB LUNCHEON

Book fans love a good ending—so they will be thrilled at the next lunch meeting when you bring out Caramel-Ice Cream Brownies for dessert. But we've gotten ahead of the story here. The meal starts with salad-stuffed cherry tomatoes and a creamy soup, followed by warm party sandwiches. The brownies arrive last, with hot Spiced Café Mocha.

## recipes

**Spiced Café Mocha**

**Caramel-Ice Cream Brownies**

**Bacon and Lettuce Stuffed Tomatoes**

**Cream of Artichoke Soup**

**Ham and Swiss Party Loaves**

**Roast Beef and Cheddar Party Loaves**

**Shown on opposite page:**
A pecan half and a drizzling of homemade caramel sauce tops off a single serving of brownies and ice cream. A dollop of whipped cream makes a fine finish for a cup of Spiced Café Mocha.

## party tips

• Don't be stuck in the kitchen while the rest of the club members get the meeting underway. A menu such as this one, using recipes that can be made ahead, will ensure that the host or hostess still has plenty of time to participate.

• One way to divide up the group's time is to encourage general socializing during the meal and to start the book discussion once the dessert is served. Guests are then free to linger over the special treat.

• You may also want to plan on supplementing the refreshments with a snack mix or chips and dip. This is especially true if the meeting includes showing a movie based on the book.

• Depending on the book selection, it might be fun to let your menu be inspired by events in the story. Use your imagination, or check online for ideas from other book clubs. Some readers even enjoy coming in book costume.

Spiced Café Mocha

Caramel-Ice Cream Brownies

# spiced café mocha

In a coffee filter or filter basket, place ground coffee, cinnamon sticks, and cloves. Add water to coffeemaker; allow to brew.

Stir chocolate syrup, sugar, and anise into brewed coffee. Pour into mugs. Garnish, if desired.

**YIELD:** about 8 cups

$^3/_4$ cup ground coffee

4 cinnamon sticks (each 3 inches)

1$^1/_2$ teaspoons whole cloves

8 cups water

$^1/_4$ cup chocolate syrup

$^1/_2$ cup sugar

$^1/_2$ teaspoon anise extract

**GARNISH:** whipped cream

# caramel-ice cream brownies

*Caramel sauce is best if made early in the day and chilled.*

For caramel sauce, combine sugar and water in a heavy large saucepan over medium heat. Stir constantly until sugar dissolves. Using a pastry brush dipped in hot water, wash down any sugar crystals on sides of pan. Increase heat to medium-high. Swirling pan occasionally, cook without stirring until syrup is dark golden brown (about 10 minutes). Remove from heat.

Using a long-handled whisk, slowly whisk in whipping cream. Return to medium heat. Whisking constantly, cook about 3 minutes or until color darkens. (Sauce will thicken as it cools.) Pour sauce into a heatproof container. Cool to room temperature. Cover and store in refrigerator.

Spread ice cream into a 9-inch square baking pan. Cover and freeze 4 hours or until firm.

For brownies, cream butter and brown sugar in a large bowl until fluffy. Add eggs and vanilla; beat until smooth. In a small bowl, combine flour, baking powder, and salt. Add dry ingredients to creamed mixture; stir until well blended. Stir in chopped pecans. Spread batter into a greased 9-inch square baking pan. Bake in a preheated 350° oven for 33 to 38 minutes or until crust starts to pull away from sides of pan. Cool in pan. Cut into 2-inch squares.

To serve, place brownies on serving plates. Cut ice cream into 2-inch squares. Place ice cream squares on brownies. Spoon caramel sauce over ice cream. Garnish, if desired.

**YIELD:** about 16 servings

## CARAMEL SAUCE
- 2 cups sugar
- 1/2 cup water
- 1 1/2 cups whipping cream

## ICE CREAM
- 1 quart vanilla ice cream, softened

## BROWNIES
- 1/3 cup butter or margarine, softened
- 1 1/2 cups firmly packed brown sugar
- 2 eggs
- 1 1/4 teaspoons vanilla extract
- 1 1/3 cups all-purpose flour
- 1 teaspoon baking powder
- 1/8 teaspoon salt
- 1 cup chopped pecans, toasted
- GARNISH: toasted pecan halves

Each of these little Bacon and Lettuce Stuffed Tomatoes is like a bite-size mini salad! The Cream of Artichoke Soup has a chicken-broth base featuring carrots, onion, and celery.

# bacon and lettuce stuffed tomatoes

Cut the top off of each tomato. Scoop out and discard pulp and seeds. Salt inside of each tomato. Invert tomatoes on paper towels and drain 15 minutes.

In a small bowl, combine lettuce, mayonnaise, bacon, green onions, salt, and pepper. Fill each tomato with mixture.

**YIELD:** 20 stuffed appetizers

20 cherry tomatoes

Salt

½ cup finely chopped lettuce

⅓ cup mayonnaise

10 slices bacon, cooked and crumbled

¼ cup chopped green onions

Salt and pepper to taste

# cream of artichoke soup

In a Dutch oven, combine oil and butter over medium heat; stir until butter melts. Sauté onion and celery in oil mixture until onion is translucent. Stir in chicken broth, artichokes, carrot, lemon juice, salt, and white pepper. Cover and cook about 30 minutes or until vegetables are tender. Remove from heat.

Purée vegetables in batches in a food processor. Return to Dutch oven. Stir in half and half and cheese. Serve warm. Garnish, if desired.

**YIELD:** about 8 cups

2 tablespoons olive oil

2 tablespoons butter

1 cup chopped onion

½ cup chopped celery

2 cans (14½ ounces each) chicken broth

2 cans (14 ounces each) artichoke hearts, drained and chopped

1 large carrot, sliced

2 tablespoons freshly squeezed lemon juice

½ teaspoon salt

½ teaspoon ground white pepper

1 cup half and half

¼ cup freshly grated Parmesan cheese

**GARNISHES:** sour cream and grated carrots

Club members can take their pick of two party loaves, served warm in narrow slices that are easy to eat when one hand is busy holding a book. Both sandwiches are dressed with fresh Dijon-style mustard spreads.

# ham and swiss party loaves

In a small bowl, combine butter, mustard, Worcestershire sauce, and onion until well blended. Split loaves in half lengthwise. Spread inside of each half with butter mixture. Layer bottom half with ham and cheese. Replace top. Wrap in aluminum foil and store in refrigerator until ready to serve.

To serve, bake loaf in foil in a 350° oven for 15 to 20 minutes or until bread is warm and cheese is melted. Cut into 1-inch slices and use toothpicks to hold sandwiches together; serve warm.

**YIELD:** about 12 servings

- ½ cup butter softened
- 3 tablespoons Dijon-style mustard
- 2 tablespoons Worcestershire sauce
- 1½ tablespoons dried minced onion
- 1 loaf (16 ounces) long narrow whole grain bread
- 8 ounces thinly sliced ham
- 6 ounces thinly sliced Swiss cheese

# roast beef and cheddar party loaves

In a small bowl, combine mayonnaise, mustard, Worcestershire sauce, and onion until well blended. Split loaf in half lengthwise. Spread inside of each half with mayonnaise mixture. Layer bottom half with roast beef and cheese. Replace top. Wrap in aluminum foil and store in refrigerator until ready to serve.

To serve, bake loaf in foil in a 350° oven for 15 to 20 minutes or until bread is warm and cheese is melted. Cut into 1-inch slices and use toothpicks to hold sandwiches together; serve warm.

**YIELD:** about 12 servings

- ⅓ cup mayonnaise
- 3 tablespoons Dijon-style mustard
- 2½ tablespoons Worcestershire sauce
- 1 tablespoon dried minced onion
- 1 loaf (16 ounces) long narrow sour dough bread
- 8 ounces thinly sliced roast beef
- 6 ounces thinly sliced Cheddar cheese

# GIRLS' NIGHT PASTA PARTY

Mamma mia! What a party it will be when all your best girlfriends get together! Hungry for news and new tastes, they are sure to enjoy this sampling of pastas and sauces, topped off with a luscious dessert of Cookies 'N' Cream Cake.

## recipes

**Sparkling Lime Spritzers**

**Alfredo Mushroom Sauce**

**Spinach Pasta Sauce**

**Marinara Sauce**

**Hearts of Lettuce with Caesar Dressing**

**Pepper and Olive Crostini**

**Cookies 'N' Cream Cake**

**Shown on opposite page:**
Encourage guests to take a sampling of all three offerings: Alfredo Mushroom Sauce on spinach fettucine (front, right); Marinara Sauce on bow tie pasta (left); and Spinach Pasta Sauce on tortellini. Sparkling Lime Spritzer is a cool and refreshing beverage.

## party tips

• Casual conversations call for comfy, cushioned furniture where people can relax. Use your dining table to set up all the foods and drinks, but invite guests to fill up individual party trays and enjoy "take-out" on the sofa or patio.

• Encourage guests to settle into a comfy spot, mingle awhile, and then move on to visit with others. To help things along, ask them to swap seats every time you ring a bell.

• To simplify party-day preparations, make the pasta ahead of time. Rinse under cold water to stop the cooking process and toss lightly with 1 to 2 teaspoons of vegetable oil to prevent sticking; cover and chill up to 4 days, or freeze up to 6 months. To reheat, place cooked pasta in a colander and run hot water over it. Or drop the pasta in boiling water, let stand for 1 to 2 minutes, and drain.

• Uncooked pasta of similar sizes and shapes may be substituted in recipes, using the same specified weight.

Sparkling Lime Spritzers

Spinach Pasta Sauce
Alfredo Mushroom Sauce

Marinara Sauce

# sparkling lime spritzers

In a small bowl, combine water and gelatin; stir until gelatin dissolves. In a 3-quart container, combine gelatin mixture, wine, vodka, and lime juice. Cover and refrigerate until well chilled.

Stir in ginger ale. Serve over ice. Garnish, if desired.

**YIELD:** about fifteen 6-ounce servings

- 2 cups boiling water
- ¼ cup lime-flavored gelatin
- 1 liter dry white wine
- 1 cup vodka
- 2 tablespoons lime juice
- 1 liter ginger ale, chilled
- **GARNISH:** lime slices

# alfredo mushroom sauce

In a large skillet, melt butter over medium heat. Add onions, garlic, salt, and pepper; cook until onions are tender. Stir in flour; cook 1 minute. Add mushrooms; cook until all liquid has evaporated. Gradually stir in cream and Parmesan cheese. Stirring constantly, bring to a boil and cook until thickened. Serve warm over fettucine.

**YIELD:** 8 to 10 servings

- ½ cup butter or margarine
- ½ cup chopped green onions
- 3 garlic cloves, minced
- 1 teaspoon salt
- ½ teaspoon pepper
- 2 tablespoons all-purpose flour
- 8 ounces fresh mushrooms, sliced
- 2 cups whipping cream, warmed
- 1 cup shredded Parmesan cheese
- 1 pound spinach fettucine, cooked according to package directions, to serve

# spinach pasta sauce

In a Dutch oven, melt butter over medium heat. Add onion and garlic; cook until onion is tender. Stir in flour; cook 1 minute. Stir in spinach, Parmesan cheese, basil, salt, and pepper. Gradually stir in broth and cream. Stirring constantly, bring to a boil and cook until thickened. Serve warm over tortellini.

YIELD: 10 to 12 servings

- 1/2 cup butter or margarine
- 1 onion, chopped
- 2 garlic cloves, minced
- 5 tablespoons all-purpose flour
- 2 packages (10 ounces each) frozen chopped spinach, thawed and well drained
- 1/3 cup shredded Parmesan cheese
- 1/4 cup chopped fresh basil leaves or 2 teaspoons dried basil leaves
- 1 teaspoon salt
- 1 teaspoon pepper
- 2 cans (14 1/2 ounces each) chicken broth
- 1/2 cup whipping cream
- 4 packages (9 ounces each) refrigerated cheese-filled tortellini, cooked according to package directions, to serve

# marinara sauce

In a large saucepan, combine oil, red pepper, onion, and garlic. Cook over medium heat until onion is tender. Add tomato sauce and next 9 ingredients; stir until well blended. Bring to a boil; reduce heat to low, cover, and simmer 1 hour. Serve warm over bow tie pasta.

YIELD: 10 to 12 servings

- 1/4 cup olive oil
- 1 cup finely chopped sweet red pepper
- 1 onion, finely chopped
- 2 garlic cloves, minced
- 1 can (29 ounces) tomato sauce
- 1 can (14 1/2 ounces) Italian-style stewed tomatoes, undrained
- 1 can (6 ounces) tomato paste
- 2 teaspoons salt
- 1 teaspoon dried parsley flakes
- 1 teaspoon sugar
- 1/2 teaspoon dried oregano leaves
- 1/2 teaspoon dried basil leaves
- 1/2 teaspoon dried thyme leaves
- 1/4 teaspoon pepper
- 1 1/2 pounds bow tie pasta, cooked according to package directions, to serve

Start the meal with a simple salad that will tantalize taste buds. The excitement comes from the homemade dressing, which you make ahead so the flavors can blend overnight. Seasoned croutons double the pleasure.

# hearts of lettuce with caesar dressing

For dressing, combine all ingredients in a 1-quart jar with a tight-fitting lid. Shake until well blended. Refrigerate 8 hours or overnight to allow flavors to blend.

For croutons, combine butter, garlic powder, and salt in a large skillet. Cook over medium heat until butter melts. Stir in bread cubes. Spread evenly on a jellyroll pan. Stirring occasionally, bake at 350° for 20 to 25 minutes or until bread is golden brown. Transfer to paper towels to cool completely.

For salad, cut heads of lettuce lengthwise into eight 1-inch slices. Place slices of lettuce on individual plates. Arrange green onions, tomatoes, and parsley on lettuce. Pour dressing over salads. Sprinkle croutons over salads.

YIELD: 8 servings

## DRESSING

- 1$2/3$ cups olive oil
- 1 cup (4 ounces) shredded Parmesan cheese
- $2/3$ cup white wine vinegar
- 1 tube (1$3/4$ ounces) anchovy paste
- 2 tablespoons lemon juice
- 3 garlic cloves, minced
- 2 teaspoons Worcestershire sauce
- 1 teaspoon salt
- 1 teaspoon pepper
- $1/2$ teaspoon dry mustard

## CROUTONS

- 1 cup butter or margarine
- 1 teaspoon garlic powder
- $1/2$ teaspoon salt
- $1/2$ loaf French bread, cut into cubes (about 4$3/4$ cups)

## SALAD

- 2 heads iceberg lettuce
- 8 green onions
- 8 cherry tomatoes, halved
  Fresh parsley

Perfect appetizers for an Italian dinner, Pepper and Olive Crostini are oven-toasted slices of French bread, spread with a marinated mixture of roasted red and green peppers, stuffed green olives, minced red onion, and tangy capers.

# pepper and olive crostini

*To save time, use purchased crostini.*

For topping, prepare peppers for roasting by cutting in half lengthwise and removing seeds and membranes. Place, skin side up, on an ungreased baking sheet; flatten with hand. Broil about 3 inches from heat for 15 to 20 minutes or until peppers are blackened and charred. Immediately seal peppers in a plastic bag and allow to steam for 10 to 15 minutes. Remove charred skin. Cut peppers into thin 2$^1/_2$-inch-long strips. Combine peppers, olives, onion, capers, oil, and vinegar in a medium bowl.

For crostini, combine oil, butter, and garlic in a small saucepan over medium-low heat; heat about 7 minutes or until butter melts. Brush butter mixture on both sides of French bread slices and place on an ungreased baking sheet. Bake at 300° for 10 to 12 minutes or until light golden and crisp.

Spread topping mixture over warm bread slices and serve immediately.

**YIELD:** about 44 slices

**TOPPING**

- 2 large green peppers
- 2 large sweet red peppers
- 1 jar (5.75 ounces) stuffed green olives, drained and sliced
- 2 tablespoons minced red onion
- 1 tablespoon drained capers
- 2 tablespoons olive oil
- 1 tablespoon balsamic vinegar

**CROSTINI**

- $^1/_4$ cup olive oil
- $^1/_4$ cup butter
- 1 garlic clove, minced
- 2 loaves 2$^1/_2$-inch-diameter French bread, sliced into $^1/_2$-inch slices

You don't have to bake all day to create this irresistible Cookies 'N' Cream Cake. Simply add crushed bits of chocolate sandwich cookies to a plain white cake mix. Decorating the cream cheese icing with cookie pieces hints that there is something special inside.

# cookies 'n' cream cake

For cake, combine cake mix, water, oil, and egg whites in a large bowl. Beat at low speed of an electric mixer 30 seconds. Beat at medium speed 2 minutes. Stir in 1 cup crushed cookies by hand. Pour batter into 2 greased and floured 9-inch round cake pans. Bake in a preheated 350° oven for 20 to 25 minutes or until a toothpick inserted in center of cake comes out clean. Cool in pans 15 minutes. Remove from pans and cool completely on a wire rack.

For icing, beat cream cheese and butter in a medium bowl until fluffy. Stir in confectioners sugar, vanilla, and enough milk for desired spreading consistency; beat until smooth.

Place 1 cake layer, top side down, on a serving plate; spread about one-fourth of icing over cake layer. Top with remaining cake layer. Spread remaining icing on top and sides of cake. Sprinkle remaining 1/2 cup crushed cookies on top of cake. Garnish, if desired. Store in refrigerator.

YIELD: 12 to 14 servings

## CAKE

- 1 package (18.25 ounces) white cake mix
- 1 1/4 cups water
- 1/3 cup vegetable oil
- 3 egg whites
- 1 1/2 cups coarsely crushed chocolate sandwich cookies (about 14 cookies), divided

## ICING

- 1 package (3 ounces) cream cheese, softened
- 2 tablespoons butter or margarine, softened
- 3 cups confectioners sugar
- 1/2 teaspoon vanilla extract
- 2 to 3 tablespoons milk

GARNISH: chocolate sandwich cookie halves

# WINE & CHEESE PARTY

Wine and cheese parties are favorites for their simplicity, versatility, and spontaneity. Preparation is easy, and invitations can be impromptu. Don't worry about following what some people consider "the rules." What matters most is what tastes good to you and your friends. Life is an adventure!

## recipes

**Four-Layer Cheese Loaf**

**Raspberry Wine**

**Spiced Apple Wine**

**Orange-Tangerine Wine**

**Cheesy Herb Pretzels**

**Caesar Snack Mix**

**Artichoke and Roasted Red Pepper Dip**

**Hot Berry-Brandy Punch**

**Raspberry Punch**

**Caramel Mocha**

**Shown on opposite page:**
Four-Layer Cheese Loaf with assorted crackers is a good hearty appetizer for this event. To spice up the wine-sampling, offer fruity choices such as Raspberry Wine, mellow Spiced Apple Wine, and Orange-Tangerine Wine.

## party tips

• Browse the Internet, library, or bookstores for advice on which types of wines and cheeses go best together. However, be aware that opinions will vary, so let your personal preferences guide your selections.

• For a good flow of guests and to avoid bottlenecks, set up serving stations throughout the room (or rooms).

• Whether to cleanse the palate or to take the edge off empty stomachs, provide an assortment of good quality crackers and breads. Go for hearty textures but avoid strong flavors that will conflict with the drinks and appetizers being served.

• Other foods that mix well with wine and cheese are fresh fruits and toasted nuts.

Four-Layer Cheese Loaf

Raspberry Wine

Spiced Apple Wine
Orange-Tangerine Wine

# four-layer cheese loaf

*To make two cheese loaves, use two 3 x 7¹/₂-inch loaf pans. Mix ingredients as directed; divide mixtures in half, and follow layering procedure for each loaf. May be frozen up to one month.*

Line a 5 x 9-inch loaf pan with heavy-duty plastic wrap, extending plastic over sides of pan; set aside.

Combine Cheddar cheese, pecans, and mayonnaise; spread half of mixture evenly into prepared pan. Combine spinach, 1 package cream cheese, salt, and pepper; spread evenly over Cheddar cheese layer. Combine remaining package cream cheese, chutney, and nutmeg; spread evenly over spinach layer. Top with remaining Cheddar cheese mixture. Cover and chill thoroughly. Use plastic wrap to remove loaf from pan. Serve chilled with assorted crackers.

**YIELD:** about 25 appetizer servings

4 cups (16 ounces) shredded sharp Cheddar cheese

¹/₂ cup chopped pecans, toasted

¹/₂ cup mayonnaise

1 package (10 ounces) frozen chopped spinach, thawed and squeezed dry

2 packages (8 ounces each) cream cheese, softened and divided

¹/₄ teaspoon salt

¹/₂ teaspoon pepper

¹/₄ cup chutney

¹/₄ teaspoon ground nutmeg

Assorted crackers to serve

# raspberry wine

In a large bowl, combine raspberries and sugar, stirring until well coated. Add wine; stir until sugar dissolves. Cover and chill 5 days.

Strain wine through a fine sieve; discard raspberries or save for another use. Serve wine chilled.

YIELD: about 3 cups

3 cups frozen unsweetened raspberries, thawed

1/4 cup sugar

1 bottle (750 ml) dry white wine

# spiced apple wine

Combine apples, sugar, and water in a large saucepan. Cook over medium-low heat about 3 minutes or until sugar dissolves. Place spices in a small square of cheesecloth and tie with kitchen string. Add spice bundle and wine to apple mixture; cook 5 minutes longer. Remove from heat and allow to cool.

Place in a covered nonmetal container in refrigerator 2 to 4 weeks. Strain wine and serve chilled.

YIELD: about 4 cups

3 medium unpeeled cooking apples, cored and finely chopped (about 4 cups)

1 cup sugar

2 tablespoons water

3 cinnamon sticks, broken into pieces

4 whole cloves

3 cardamom pods, crushed

1 bottle (750 ml) dry white wine

# orange-tangerine wine

Combine water and sugar in a small saucepan. Stirring constantly, cook over medium heat until sugar dissolves. In a 1-gallon container, combine wine, juice concentrates, liqueur, and sugar mixture. Stir until well blended. Serve chilled.

YIELD: about 9 cups

1 cup water

1/2 cup sugar

1 bottle (1.5 liters) dry white wine

1/4 cup frozen orange juice concentrate, thawed

1/4 cup frozen tangerine juice concentrate, thawed

1/2 cup orange-flavored liqueur

Adventurous guests will appreciate the wide range of tastes and textures in Caesar Snack Mix and Cheesy Herb Pretzels.

# caesar snack mix

Place crackers, croutons, and breadstick pieces in a large roasting pan; set aside.

In a medium bowl, whisk oil, melted butter, Parmesan cheese, lemon juice, garlic, mustard, Worcestershire sauce, parsley, salt, and white pepper until well blended. Pour over cracker mixture; toss until well coated.

Bake at 250° for 1 hour, stirring every 15 minutes. Spread on aluminum foil to cool.

**YIELD:** about 20 cups

- 1 package (14 ounces) oyster crackers
- 1 package (7 ounces) rye chip crackers
- 2 packages (6 ounces each) plain croutons
- 1 package ($3^{1}/_{4}$ ounces) pencil-size plain breadsticks (grissini), broken into 1-inch pieces
- $^{1}/_{2}$ cup olive oil
- $^{1}/_{2}$ cup butter or margarine, melted
- $^{1}/_{2}$ cup freshly grated Parmesan cheese
- 6 tablespoons freshly squeezed lemon juice
- 6 garlic cloves, minced
- 2 tablespoons Dijon-style mustard
- 2 tablespoons Worcestershire sauce
- 2 tablespoons parsley flakes
- $^{1}/_{2}$ teaspoon salt
- $^{1}/_{2}$ teaspoon ground white pepper

# cheesy herb pretzels

Place pretzels in a large bowl; set aside.

In a medium saucepan, melt butter over medium heat. Remove from heat; stir in Parmesan cheese, sauce mix, dressing mix, and garlic powder. Pour over pretzels; stir until well coated.

Spread pretzels on 2 ungreased baking sheets. Bake at 350° for 10 to 12 minutes or until golden brown. Cool completely on baking sheets.

**YIELD:** about $15^{1}/_{2}$ cups

- 14 cups (about 20 ounces) small pretzels
- 1 cup butter or margarine
- 1 cup grated Parmesan cheese
- 3 packages (1.6 ounces each) garlic and herb sauce mix
- 2 packages (1 ounce each) ranch-style salad dressing mix
- 1 teaspoon garlic powder

For gourmet tastes, serve Artichoke and Roasted Red Pepper Dip. It goes superbly with a variety of hearty crackers, chips, and mini toast rounds.

# artichoke and roasted red pepper dip

To roast sweet red peppers, cut in half lengthwise and remove seeds and membranes. Place, skin side up, on an ungreased baking sheet; flatten peppers with hand. Broil about 3 inches from heat about 10 minutes or until peppers are blackened. Immediately seal peppers in a plastic bag and allow to steam 10 to 15 minutes. Remove and discard charred skin; coarsely chop peppers.

In a medium skillet over medium heat, cook green onions in butter until tender. Remove from heat. Stir in artichoke hearts, 1 cup Parmesan cheese, mayonnaise, sour cream, salt, ground red pepper, and roasted peppers. Spoon into a greased 1-quart baking dish. Sprinkle with remaining $1/4$ cup Parmesan cheese. Bake, uncovered, at 350° for 25 minutes or until heated through. Serve warm with crackers or bread.

**YIELD:** about $3^1/4$ cups

- 2 large sweet red peppers
- $1/4$ cup sliced green onions
- 2 tablespoons butter or margarine
- 1 can (14 ounces) artichoke hearts, drained and chopped
- $1^1/4$ cups freshly grated Parmesan cheese, divided
- 1 cup mayonnaise
- $1/2$ cup sour cream
- $1/4$ teaspoon salt
- $1/8$ teaspoon ground red pepper
  Crackers or toasted bread to serve

A selection of hot drinks and mild refreshments provides a rich closure for such a delicious experience.

# hot berry-brandy punch

In a blender or food processor, purée raspberries. Strain; discard seeds and pulp. In a Dutch oven, combine raspberry purée, cranberry juice, and sugar; bring to a simmer, stirring until sugar dissolves. Stir in brandy and liqueur. Serve warm.

YIELD: about twenty-six 6-ounce servings

- 2 packages (12 ounces each) frozen raspberries, thawed
- 1 gallon cranberry juice cocktail
- 2 cups sugar
- 2 cups blackberry-flavored brandy
- 1/2 cup raspberry-flavored liqueur

# raspberry punch

In a punch bowl, stir together pineapple juice, drink mixer, orange juice concentrate, club soda, and soft drink. Stir in raspberries; serve chilled.

YIELD: about twenty-four 6-ounce servings

- 1 can (46 ounces) unsweetened pineapple juice, chilled
- 2 cups piña colada drink mixer, chilled
- 1 can (12 ounces) frozen orange juice concentrate, thawed
- 1 liter club soda, chilled
- 1 liter lemon-lime soft drink, chilled
- 1 package (10 ounces) frozen raspberries in syrup, slightly thawed

# caramel mocha

In a small Dutch oven, combine sweetened condensed milk, caramel topping, and chocolate syrup. Stirring constantly, cook over medium-low heat about 8 minutes or until mixture is well blended and hot. Add coffee; stir until blended. Serve hot.

YIELD: about 12 cups

- 1 can (14 ounces) sweetened condensed milk
- 1 jar (12 ounces) caramel ice cream topping
- 1/2 cup chocolate-flavored syrup
- 2 1/2 quarts hot, strongly brewed coffee

# GAME WATCH

Got the guys coming over to watch the big game? Here's a bold meal that they will tackle with gusto! Make-Ahead Saucy Ribs are finger-licking good, and they team up great with spicy potatoes and baked beans. For pre-game snacking, hand off a crunchy popcorn mix and a robust cheese to spread on hearty crackers. Coconut Candy Bar Cake makes an all-star dessert. Touchdown!

## recipes

**Field Goal Potatoes**
**Make-Ahead Saucy Ribs**
**Baked Bean Blitz**
**Savory Snack Mix**
**Beer Cheese Spread**
**Coconut Candy Bar Cake**

**Shown on opposite page:**
Because most of the preparation can be done the night before, Make-Ahead Saucy Ribs are a great party choice. Score extra points with cheesy Field Goal Potatoes and Baked Bean Blitz!

## party tips

• While the game is in play, all eyes will be on the TV screen, so don't worry about party décor—other than to use the home team's colors, of course!

• With all that screaming and yelling, parched throats will need a steady supply of cold drinks, and energy levels will need to be replenished frequently with handfuls of chips and other munchables.

• Beverage planning is easy. Simply stock up on the gang's favorite brew or soft drinks, and put on a pot of coffee to go with dessert.

• Serve the meal and snacks buffet-style, and set out an assortment of sturdy plates and bowls that can be filled and taken into the huddle. Also plan on using strategically placed platters that the guys can intercept easily for refills.

• For fans who like to kick up the flavor, provide a selection of spicy herb blends, hot sauces, and other condiments.

Field Goal Potatoes

Make-Ahead Saucy Ribs

Baked Bean Blitz

# field goal potatoes

Place potatoes in a large bowl. In a small bowl, whisk oil and cheese sauce mix until well blended. Stir green chiles, onion, cumin, garlic powder, salt, and cilantro into cheese mixture. Pour mixture over potatoes, stirring until potatoes are well coated.

Spread potato mixture in a single layer in a greased $10^{1}/_{2}$ x $15^{1}/_{2}$-inch jellyroll pan. Bake at 400° for 35 to 45 minutes or until potatoes are tender and golden brown. Serve warm.

YIELD: about 12 servings

3 pounds unpeeled red potatoes, cut into chunks

6 tablespoons vegetable oil

2 packages ($1^{1}/_{4}$ ounces each) cheese sauce mix

1 can (4.5 ounces) chopped green chiles

3 tablespoons dried minced onion

1 tablespoon ground cumin

1 tablespoon garlic powder

$1^{1}/_{2}$ teaspoons salt

$^{3}/_{4}$ teaspoon dried cilantro

# make-ahead saucy ribs

Place rib racks in a single layer in foil-lined baking pans. Sprinkle ribs with salt and pepper. Cover with foil and bake at 350° for 1 hour or until fully cooked. Let cool.

While ribs are cooking, sauté onion and green pepper in oil in a large saucepan over medium heat until tender. Stir in ketchup, brown sugar, marmalade, vinegar, pepper sauce, 1 teaspoon salt, and 3/4 teaspoon black pepper. Stirring constantly, bring sauce to a simmer. Reduce heat to medium low. Stirring frequently, cook sauce 30 minutes (mixture will be thick). Remove from heat and let cool.

Cut racks into individual ribs. Transfer to a heavy-duty resealable plastic bag. Pour 2 cups sauce over ribs; refrigerate overnight to let ribs marinate. Store remaining sauce in refrigerator.

To serve, place ribs in foil-lined baking pans. Spoon sauce from plastic bag over ribs. Bake, uncovered, at 425° for 1 hour or until sauce cooks onto ribs, turning every 15 minutes and basting with remaining sauce. Serve warm.

YIELD: about 3 dozen

- 5 pounds pork loin baby back ribs
- Salt and pepper
- 1 cup finely chopped onion
- 1 cup finely chopped green pepper
- 3 tablespoons vegetable oil
- 1 bottle (28 ounces) ketchup
- 1 1/2 cups firmly packed brown sugar
- 3/4 cup orange marmalade
- 3/4 cup apple cider vinegar
- 1 tablespoon hot pepper sauce
- 1 teaspoon salt
- 3/4 teaspoon pepper

# baked bean blitz

In a large skillet, cook bacon; remove bacon and reserve drippings in skillet. Crumble bacon and set aside.

Cook onions in bacon drippings until tender. In a 9 x 13-inch baking dish, combine onions and drippings with beans, barbecue sauce, brown sugar, mustard, Worcestershire sauce, and salt. Stirring occasionally, bake at 300° for about 2 hours. To serve, stir in crumbled bacon. Serve warm.

YIELD: about 10 servings

- 6 slices bacon
- 1 cup chopped onions
- 2 cans (28 ounces each) baked beans
- 2 cans (15.3 ounces each) lima beans, drained
- 1 cup barbecue sauce
- 3/4 cup firmly packed brown sugar
- 2 tablespoons prepared mustard
- 1 tablespoon Worcestershire sauce
- 3/4 teaspoon salt

Beer Cheese Spread combines sharp and mild shredded Cheddar with bold flavorings and beer. Savory Snack Mix is jammed full of favorite munchies, including popcorn, cheese crackers, corn chips, and nuts—coated with a garlicky red pepper sauce.

# beer cheese spread

Combine cheeses, dry mustard, garlic, and red pepper in a large food processor; process just until blended. Gradually add beer through feed tube; process until well blended. Spoon into a serving container; chill. Store in refrigerator. Serve with crackers.

**YIELD:** about 6 cups

4 cups (16 ounces) shredded sharp Cheddar cheese

4 cups (16 ounces) shredded mild Cheddar cheese

1 teaspoon dry mustard

1 garlic clove, minced

1/8 teaspoon ground red pepper

1 bottle (12 ounces) beer

Crackers to serve

# savory snack mix

Combine popcorn, corn chips, crackers, and pecans in a large roasting pan. In a small saucepan, melt butter over medium-low heat. Remove from heat and stir in Worcestershire sauce, cumin, garlic salt, and red pepper. Pour over popcorn mixture; stir until well coated. Bake at 250° for 1 hour, stirring every 15 minutes. Spread on aluminum foil to cool.

**YIELD:** about 19 cups

12 cups popped popcorn

6 cups corn chips

1 package (10 ounces) cheese snack crackers

3 cups pecan halves

1 cup butter or margarine

1/4 cup Worcestershire sauce

1 tablespoon ground cumin

2 teaspoons garlic salt

1/2 teaspoon ground red pepper

Celebrate the team's victory (or console the fans after a loss!) with Coconut Candy Bar Cake. This sinfully delicious dessert can be fixed in a snap! It's made with devil's food cake mix and ready-to-spread fudge frosting but adds a sweet marshmallow-coconut filling.

# coconut candy bar cake

In a medium saucepan, combine sugar, evaporated milk, and butter over medium-high heat. Stirring frequently, bring mixture to a boil. Reduce heat to medium; continue to stir and cook 2 minutes. Remove from heat. Stir in marshmallows until melted. Stir in coconut. Chill filling 1 hour.

Cut each cake layer in half to make 4 thin layers. Spread filling evenly between layers. Spread frosting on top and sides of cake. Store in refrigerator.

**YIELD:** 12 to 14 servings

1 cup sugar

1 cup evaporated milk

½ cup butter or margarine

24 marshmallows

1 package (14 ounces) flaked coconut

2 9-inch-round devil's food cake layers (prepared from a cake mix)

1 container (16 ounces) chocolate fudge ready-to-spread frosting

# TEEN FIESTA

Teens love to turn up the volume on everything, including taste! This South of the Border fiesta treats them to hot and spicy flavors and then lets them chill out with icy fruit punch and a cake that's cool and creamy. Olé!

## recipes

**Orange-Pineapple Punch**
**Cheesy Bean Burritos**
**Mini Beef Nachos**
**Mexican Macaroni and Cheese**
**South of the Border Salsa**
**White Cheese Dip**
**Tres Leches Cake**

**Shown on opposite page:**
Ice-cold, slushy Orange-Pineapple Punch is a refreshing match for a spicy meal of Mini Beef Nachos (from left), Cheesy Bean Burritos, and Mexican Macaroni and Cheese.

## party tips

• Read through all the recipes well in advance so you can plan your timeline for preparations. Several recipes featured here provide their best flavor when made ahead, to allow for flavors to blend or for thorough chilling.

• With some recipes, you may want to prepare an additional batch so that you can offer a milder (or spicier) version.

• To keep cheese dip warm, consider using an insulated dish or a slow cooker that has a special low-heat setting.

• To mix things up, offer a variety of chips, from crisp restaurant-style to red or blue corn tortilla chips.

• So that guests can circulate among friends instead of crowding around the chips and dip table, set out a stack of small party plates that they can load up and carry along.

• The fiesta theme is easy to pull off with dishes and table linens in a mix of bold, bright colors. Toss in some fresh flowers, too.

Orange-Pineapple Punch

Mini Beef Nachos
Cheesy Bean Burritos

Mexican Macaroni and Cheese

# orange-pineapple punch

*Punch must be made 1 day before serving.*

In a 6-quart container, combine water, pineapple, sugar, bananas, orange juice concentrate, lemonade concentrate, and drink mix; freeze.

Remove punch from freezer 4 hours before serving to partially thaw.

To serve, break into chunks. Add ginger ale and jar of cherries; stir until slushy.

Garnish, if desired.

YIELD: about twenty-seven 6-ounce servings

- 2 quarts water
- 2 cans (20 ounces each) unsweetened crushed pineapple, undrained
- 3 cups sugar
- 3 ripe bananas, mashed
- 1 can (12 ounces) frozen orange juice concentrate, thawed
- 1 can (6 ounces) frozen lemonade concentrate, thawed
- 1 package (0.19 ounces) unsweetened orange-flavored soft drink mix
- 1 liter ginger ale, chilled
- 1 jar (10 ounces) maraschino cherries, drained
  GARNISH: maraschino cherries with stems

# cheesy bean burritos

In a large bowl, combine beans, shredded cheese, and green chiles. For each burrito, place 1 cheese slice on a tortilla, matching round edges. Spread about ¼ cup of bean mixture over cheese. Beginning with cheese side, roll up tortilla. Place burritos, seam side down, in 2 lightly greased 9 x 13-inch baking pans. Cover with aluminum foil. Bake at 325° for 40 to 45 minutes or until burritos are heated through and cheese melts. Serve warm with salsa and sour cream.

YIELD: 20

- 3 cans (16 ounces each) refried beans
- 2 cups (8 ounces) shredded Monterey Jack cheese with jalapeño peppers
- 1 can (4.5 ounces) chopped green chiles
- 20 slices (about 16 ounces) half-moon-shaped Monterey Jack cheese with jalapeño peppers
- 2 packages (10 count each) 7-inch flour tortillas
  Salsa and sour cream to serve

# mini beef nachos

In a small saucepan, combine beans, chili powder, and cumin. Cook, stirring occasionally, over medium-low heat until heated through. Remove from heat and cover.

In a large skillet, over medium heat, cook beef and onion until beef is done and onion is tender. Stir in chiles, cilantro, salt, and pepper. Remove from heat and stir in tomato.

Spread about 1 teaspoon bean mixture evenly over each tortilla chip; place in a single layer on a greased baking pan. Spoon about 1 tablespoon beef mixture over bean mixture. Sprinkle cheese evenly over beef mixture. Bake at 425° for 5 to 7 minutes or until cheese melts. Serve warm.

**YIELD:** about 4$\frac{1}{2}$ dozen

- 1 can (16 ounces) regular or vegetarian refried beans
- 1 teaspoon chili powder
- 1 teaspoon ground cumin
- 1$\frac{1}{2}$ pounds ground beef
- $\frac{1}{2}$ cup chopped onion
- 1 can (4.5 ounces) chopped green chiles
- 2 tablespoons chopped fresh cilantro
- 1 teaspoon salt
- $\frac{1}{2}$ teaspoon pepper
- 1 cup finely chopped tomato (about 1 large tomato)
- 1 bag (10$\frac{1}{2}$ ounces) round tortilla chips
- 2 cups (8 ounces) shredded Monterey Jack cheese

# mexican macaroni and cheese

In a large bowl, combine cooked macaroni, kidney beans, tomatoes, green chiles, ripe olives, and cilantro. Melt butter in a large saucepan over medium heat. Sauté green onions in butter just until tender. Remove from heat. Use a slotted spoon to transfer onions to macaroni mixture.

Return butter to medium heat; whisk flour into butter until well blended and mixture begins to bubble. Stirring constantly, add warm milk; cook about 6 minutes or until smooth and slightly thickened. Remove from heat and add 3 cups cheese; stir until melted. Stir in cumin, garlic salt, and red pepper. Pour over macaroni mixture.

Spoon into a greased 9 x 13-inch baking dish. Sprinkle remaining 1 cup cheese over top. Cover and bake at 350° for 30 minutes. Uncover and bake for 10 minutes longer or until mixture is bubbly.

**YIELD:** about 14 servings

- 1 package (12 ounces) large elbow macaroni, cooked
- 1 can (16 ounces) dark red kidney beans, drained
- 1 can (14.5 ounces) stewed tomatoes, drained
- 1 can (4.5 ounces) chopped green chiles
- 1 can (4$\frac{1}{4}$ ounces) chopped ripe olives
- $\frac{1}{3}$ cup chopped fresh cilantro
- $\frac{1}{4}$ cup butter or margarine
- $\frac{1}{3}$ cup finely chopped green onions
- 3 tablespoons all-purpose flour
- 2$\frac{1}{4}$ cups warm milk
- 4 cups (16 ounces) shredded Cheddar cheese, divided
- 1 teaspoon ground cumin
- $\frac{1}{4}$ teaspoon garlic salt
- $\frac{1}{8}$ teaspoon ground red pepper

Take the edge off of teens' never-ending appetites with chips and dips. South of the Border Salsa makes a zesty snack, while White Cheese Dip is hearty and filling.

# south of the border salsa

Combine tomatoes, oil, parsley, onion, peppers, and garlic in a non-metallic container. Refrigerate overnight to allow flavors to blend.

Serve with tortilla chips.

**YIELD:** about 3 cups

- 1 can (28 ounces) whole tomatoes with liquid, chopped
- 1/2 cup olive oil
- 1/2 cup minced fresh parsley
- 1 medium onion, minced
- 1/4 cup chopped jalapeño peppers
- 2 garlic cloves, minced
  Tortilla chips to serve

# white cheese dip

In a large saucepan, melt butter over medium heat. Stir in flour, cumin, garlic salt, and dry mustard. Stirring constantly, cook 1 minute. Gradually stir in half and half. Stirring constantly, cook about 5 minutes or until mixture thickens. Stir in peppers, pepper juice, and cheese. Cook until cheese melts and mixture is smooth.

Serve warm with tortilla chips.

**YIELD:** about 3 cups

- 1/4 cup butter or margarine
- 1/4 cup all-purpose flour
- 1 tablespoon ground cumin
- 1 teaspoon garlic salt
- 1/4 teaspoon dry mustard
- 2 cups half and half
- 2 tablespoons chopped pickled jalapeño peppers
- 2 teaspoons juice from pickled jalapeño peppers
- 2 cups (8 ounces) shredded white American cheese
  Tortilla chips to serve

Want to enrich the party with a quick lesson in Spanish? Serve Tres Leches Cake and explain how it is named for the three milks that make it so rich and moist. The tender cake is soaked in the creamy syrup and then topped with whipped cream and fruit.

# tres leches cake

*A Mexican favorite, this moist, dense cake is named for the three milks in which it is soaked (in Spanish, tres means three and leche is milk).*

Lightly grease and flour a 9 x 13-inch baking dish; set aside.

For cream syrup, whisk together condensed milk, evaporated milk, and whipping cream in a medium bowl until well blended. Chill in refrigerator while cake is baking and cooling.

For cake, combine flour, baking powder, and salt in a medium bowl. In a large mixing bowl, cream butter and sugar until fluffy. Add eggs, one at a time, and vanilla; beat until foamy. Alternately fold in dry ingredients and milk with a spatula until batter is smooth; do not overmix. Pour batter into prepared baking dish. Bake in a preheated 350° oven for 25 to 30 minutes or until a toothpick inserted in center of cake comes out clean and cake begins to pull away from sides of dish. Allow cake to cool to room temperature in dish on a wire rack.

Turn out cake onto a serving plate with a rim. Pierce top of cake with a fork; cover with plastic wrap and chill in refrigerator for 30 minutes. When cake is cool, pour cream syrup evenly over cake, a little at a time, until cake is saturated. (You may not need entire amount of syrup at this time, but reserve for later use.) Cover and refrigerate saturated cake for at least 1 hour, occasionally spooning reserved syrup on cake. Keep chilled until ready to serve.

For whipped cream, beat whipping cream in a large chilled bowl until cream begins to thicken. Add sugar and vanilla; continue beating until stiff peaks form. (You may want to remove edges of cake for a nicer appearance.) Using a spatula, spread whipped cream over top of cake. Garnish, if desired. Store in refrigerator.

**YIELD:** about 15 servings

## CREAM SYRUP

- 1 can (14 ounces) sweetened condensed milk
- 1 can (12 ounces) evaporated milk
- 1/2 cup whipping cream

## CAKE

- 1 1/2 cups all-purpose flour
- 1 teaspoon baking powder
- 1/2 teaspoon salt
- 1/2 cup butter, softened
- 1 cup sugar
- 5 eggs
- 1 teaspoon vanilla extract
- 1/2 cup milk

## WHIPPED CREAM

- 1 cup whipping cream
- 1 tablespoon sugar
- 1 teaspoon vanilla extract

**GARNISHES: crushed pineapple and maraschino cherries**

# HALLOWEEN

"Trick or treat! Give me something good to eat!" Invite your favorite ghouls over on Halloween for a lively monster mash, and you'll hear this playful greeting time after time. When those hungry hobgoblins come a-haunting, bewitch them with eerie edibles dressed up like grinning jack-o'-lanterns and friendly ghosts. They'll love it if you also hand out some of the treats in fun bags they can take home at the end of the night.

## recipes

**Ghost Cookies**
**Jack-O'-Lantern Cookies**
**Pumpkin Dip**
**Spicy Jack-O'-Lantern Punch**
**Jack-O'-Lantern Cheese Spread**
**Candy Pumpkin Snack Mix**
**Nutty Popcorn Crunch**
**Gourmet Caramel Apples**

**Shown on opposite page:**
These creepy cookies are so frightfully easy to create that you can let the kids help. Simply dress up store-bought cookies with melted confectionery coatings and decorate with candy pieces.

## party tips

• Pumpkins, gourds, autumn leaves, and other natural accents will help create a spellbinding fall look for your Halloween party.

• Turn on eerie music and set up motion-activated sound-effects at the entrance and in a few surprising spots to set a spooky mood.

• Candy and sweets are a must at Halloween get-togethers, but be sure to offer other foods to combat all that sugar. Set out plenty of nuts, crackers, cheeses, mini sandwiches, antipasto, carrot sticks, and other fresh vegetables and fruits.

• When making snack mixes, it's okay to substitute snack items that your family and friends personally love, such as cereals, mini cookies, and different types of nuts and candies.

• Creative bags are a fun way to pack up candied apples and portions of popcorn or snack mix for party favors or take-home treats (see Creative Packaging Ideas on page 70).

Ghost Cookies

Jack-O'-Lantern Cookies

# creative packaging ideas

*Creative bags and wraps are fun ways to pack up candied apples and portions of popcorn or other snack mixes for party favors or take-home treats.*

• Simply place food in a small cellophane bag, twist closed, and tie ribbon or raffia around the closing. Glue on a paper label or include a tie-on tag to share a fun rhyme or name the treat, such as "Goblin Food" or "Fright-Night Delights."

• Use paint, markers, or appliqués to decorate paper lunch bags with Halloween shapes, such as black cats and ghosts.

• Dress up orange paper cups with jack-o'-lantern faces and wrap each treat-filled cup with clear cellophane.

• For bat buckets, cut out paper or felt bat wings to glue to the sides of a plastic foam cup that has been painted black on the outside. To make a carrying handle, thread ribbon on a needle and insert through the top edge of the cup at each side; knot ribbon ends inside cup. Line the cup with a colorful napkin.

# ghost cookies

For eyes, cut jelly beans in half; set aside.

Melt candy coating following package instructions. Dip two-thirds of each cookie in melted candy, shaking gently to remove excess coating. Place on wire rack with waxed paper underneath. Place jelly beans on cookies. Allow coating to harden before removing from rack.

**YIELD:** about 32

Small black jelly beans

6 ounces vanilla-flavored candy coating

1 package (15.5 ounces) peanut-shaped peanut butter sandwich cookies

# jack-o'-lantern cookies

Spread a small amount of peanut butter on the bottom (flat side) of half of the cookies, top with remaining cookies. For faces, cut licorice into small triangles and squares.

Melt candy coating following package instructions. Remove from heat and tint with food coloring. Using tongs, dip each sandwich cookie in melted candy coating, covering completely. Gently shake each cookie to remove excess coating. Place on wire rack with waxed paper underneath. Place licorice pieces on the cookies for faces. Allow coating to harden before removing from rack.

**YIELD:** about 20

$1/2$ cup smooth peanut butter

1 package (9 ounces) chocolate wafer cookies

Black licorice candy

24 ounces vanilla-flavored candy coating

Orange paste food coloring

Lightly spiced Pumpkin Dip is delicious with gingersnaps. Serve it in a fun bowl or a small hollowed-out pumpkin. A fun, fizzy brew, the Spicy Jack-O'-Lantern Punch is prepared with fruit juices and pumpkin pie spice.

# pumpkin dip

In a large mixing bowl, combine sugar and cream cheese, beating until well blended. Beat in pumpkin pie filling mix, cinnamon, and ginger. Chill until ready to serve.

Serve with purchased gingersnaps. Store in refrigerator.

**YIELD:** about 7 cups

- 4 cups confectioners sugar
- 2 packages (8 ounces each) cream cheese, softened
- 1 can (30 ounces) pumpkin pie filling mix
- 2 teaspoons ground cinnamon
- 1 teaspoon ground ginger
  Gingersnaps to serve

# spicy jack-o'-lantern punch

In a 1$^1$/$_2$-quart container, combine juice concentrates and water. Add soft drink mix and pumpkin pie spice; whisk until well blended. Cover and chill.

Place punch mix in a 1-gallon container and add lemon-lime soda. Stir and serve immediately.

**YIELD:** about 11 cups

- 1 can (12 ounces) frozen orange juice concentrate, thawed
- 1 can (12 ounces) frozen orange-pineapple juice concentrate, thawed
- 2 cups water
- 1 package (0.15 ounces) unsweetened orange-flavored soft drink mix
- 2 teaspoons pumpkin pie spice
- 4 cans (12 ounces each) lemon-lime soda, chilled

This Jack-O'-Lantern Cheese Spread is so delicious, it's spooky! Russian-style salad dressing adds zip to a creamy blend of cheeses, and chopped black olives create the face. Party ghouls will grab up the tasty Candy Pumpkin Snack Mix, which combines mini peanut butter sandwich crackers with candy pumpkins and chocolate-covered peanuts

# jack-o'-lantern cheese spread

Line an 8-inch round cake pan with plastic wrap, extending plastic wrap over sides of pan; lightly oil plastic wrap. Process cheeses and salad dressing in a food processor until well blended. Spread cheese mixture into prepared pan. Cover and chill 2 hours or until firm.

Use ends of plastic wrap to remove cheese from pan. Invert cheese onto serving plate. Smooth top and sides of cheese with a small spatula. Use a toothpick to draw outline of eyes, nose, and mouth of jack-o'-lantern on cheese mixture. Fill in outlines with olives. Serve at room temperature with crackers. Store in refrigerator.

**YIELD:** about 3$\frac{1}{2}$ cups

- 4 cups (16 ounces) shredded sharp Cheddar cheese
- 1 package (8 ounces) cream cheese, softened
- $\frac{1}{2}$ cup Russian-style salad dressing
- 3 tablespoons chopped black olives
- Crackers to serve

# candy pumpkin snack mix

In a large bowl, combine crackers, pumpkin candies, and chocolate-covered peanuts. Store in a cool place.

**YIELD:** about 7 cups

- 1 package (7$\frac{1}{2}$ ounces) mini peanut butter sandwich crackers
- 12 ounces pumpkin-shaped candies
- 1 package (6 ounces) chocolate-covered peanuts

Here's a tasty snack that no goblin can resist! Nutty Popcorn Crunch has amaretto-flavored oil in the candy coating. Place bowls of it all around the house so guests can grab a handful to nibble as they mingle. Or see the Creative Packaging Ideas on page 70.

# nutty popcorn crunch

Combine popcorn and nuts in a large roasting pan. In a heavy large saucepan, combine brown sugar, butter, corn syrup, and salt. Stirring constantly, bring to a boil over medium heat. Boil 5 minutes without stirring. Remove from heat; stir in flavored oil and baking soda (mixture will foam).

Pour syrup over popcorn mixture; stir until well coated. Bake at 275° for 45 minutes, stirring every 15 minutes. Spread on aluminum foil to cool.

**YIELD:** about 21 cups

| | |
|---|---|
| 16 | cups popped popcorn |
| 2 | cans (10 ounces each) mixed nuts |
| 2 | cups firmly packed brown sugar |
| $1/2$ | cup butter or margarine |
| $1/2$ | cup light corn syrup |
| $1/4$ | teaspoon salt |
| $1/4$ | teaspoon amaretto-flavored oil (used in candy making) |
| $1/2$ | teaspoon baking soda |

Caramel apples become gourmet fare when dipped in white or semisweet chocolate and rolled in chopped pecans. Grown-up party ghouls will drool for these delectable sweets! Wrap some up for take-home treats or party game prizes, too.

# gourmet caramel apples

Insert craft sticks into stem ends of apples. In a medium saucepan, combine caramels and water. Stirring constantly, cook over medium-low heat until smooth. Remove from heat.

Holding each apple over saucepan, spoon caramel mixture over apples. Cool completely on greased waxed paper.

Stirring constantly, melt desired chocolate in a small saucepan over low heat. Remove from heat.

Holding each caramel-coated apple over saucepan, spoon chocolate over apple. Roll in pecans. Return to waxed paper to cool completely. Store in refrigerator.

**YIELD:** 1 dozen

12 craft sticks

6 medium Red Delicious apples

6 medium Granny Smith apples

3 bags (14 ounces each) caramel candy

6 tablespoons water

28 ounces semisweet or white baking chocolate, coarsely chopped

5 cups chopped pecans

# KIDS' CHRISTMAS

The frivolity of Christmas is meant for children, so give them their own fun holiday party, featuring delicious snacks, something creative to do, and good times to remember. They'll certainly never forget this sweet Popcorn Snowman centerpiece, which is almost as easy to make as popcorn balls. And they'll be so proud of the necklaces they make by stringing popcorn, candy, and cookies. Oh, to be a kid again!

## recipes

**Cinnamon-Apple Popcorn**
**Cherry Punch**
**Popcorn Snowman**
**Edible Necklaces**
**Snowman Gingerbread Cookies**
**Minty Marshmallow Fruit Dip**

**Shown on opposite page:**
Our Popcorn Snowman is a cute table decoration that's good to eat, too. But to keep him from getting munched away too soon, set out plenty of Cinnamon-Apple Popcorn and Cherry Punch.

## party tips

• When family and friends get together for the holidays, make sure there are special treats just for the kids, as well as creative activities to add to the fun.

• One such activity is making edible necklaces (see page 85) by stringing popcorn and candy, with a special cookie as a pendant. Adult supervision is advised, because a sharp needle will be necessary to penetrate the popcorn. If you prefer to have the kids use blunt plastic yarn needles, limit their supplies to miniature marshmallows or candies that are soft or have center holes.

• Decorating gingerbread cookies (see page 86) is another holiday activity that children traditionally enjoy. Let grown-ups bake the cookies ahead of time, but set the kids free to embellish the shapes with icing and additional candies. Don't expect perfection, but do expect perfect bliss as each child crafts cookies that are unique and delicious.

• Provide enough supplies for all the children to work at the same time, so no one has to wait. Colored icing can be divided up ahead of time by placing small amounts in plastic bags; snip one corner of each bag when the artists are ready to start decorating.

• You'll want to keep your camera handy as the kids make progress. For keepsake party favors, take pictures of the children with their completed creations.

Cinnamon-Apple Popcorn

Cherry Punch

Popcorn Snowman

# cinnamon-apple popcorn

Place apple pieces in a large shallow baking pan. Bake at 250° for 20 minutes. Remove pan from oven and stir in popcorn and pecans.

In a small bowl, combine melted butter and remaining ingredients. Drizzle butter mixture over popcorn mixture, stirring well. Bake at 250° for 30 minutes, stirring every 10 minutes. Spread on waxed paper to cool.

**YIELD:** about 14 cups

2   cups dried apple pieces
10  cups popped popcorn
2   cups pecan halves
1/4 cup butter, melted
1   teaspoon cinnamon
1/4 teaspoon nutmeg
2   tablespoons brown sugar
1/4 teaspoon vanilla extract

# cherry punch

*Make punch the day it will be served.*

In a small bowl, stir boiling water into gelatin until gelatin dissolves. In a large container, combine gelatin, lemonade concentrate, and apple juice. Cover and chill 2 hours.

To serve, stir in cherry-lemon-lime soda; serve immediately.

**YIELD:** about 7 1/2 cups

1   cup boiling water
1   package (3 ounces) cherry gelatin
1   can (6 ounces) frozen pink lemonade concentrate, thawed
3   cups apple juice
2   cans (12 ounces each) cherry-lemon-lime soda, chilled

# popcorn snowman

*Mixture sets up quickly; have someone help you shape the snowman.*

Place popcorn in a large greased roasting pan; set aside.

Butter sides of a heavy medium saucepan. Combine sugar, corn syrup, butter, cream of tartar, and salt in pan. Stirring constantly, cook over medium-high heat until mixture is fluid (about 5 minutes). Using a pastry brush dipped in hot water, wash down any sugar crystals on sides of pan. Attach a candy thermometer to pan, making sure thermometer does not touch bottom of pan. Cook, without stirring, until mixture reaches hard-ball stage (approximately 250° to 268°). Test about 1/2 teaspoon mixture in ice water. Mixture will roll into a hard ball in ice water and will remain hard when removed from the water. Remove from heat and stir in vanilla and baking soda (mixture will foam). Pour mixture over popcorn; stir until coated.

As soon as mixture is cool enough to handle, use greased hands to shape one 8-inch-diameter ball, one 6-inch-diameter ball, and one 4-inch-diameter ball; let cool. Stack balls on a plate from largest to smallest. Insert skewer through center of balls to secure.

Decorate Snowman by using white icing to attach jelly bean pieces for eyes and mouth, candy corn for nose, and gumdrop pieces for buttons. Tie fleece scarf around neck. Insert two wooden skewers into snowman for arms. Use mitten pattern and cut 4 felt mittens; glue curved edges of 2 pieces together for each mitten. Glue two small bows to mittens; slide onto skewers. Place cap on head.

**YIELD:** 13-inch-high snowman

### SNOWMAN

- 24 cups popped white popcorn
- 2 cups sugar
- 1 cup light corn syrup
- 1 tablespoon butter or margarine
- 2 teaspoons cream of tartar
- 3/4 teaspoon salt
- 1 teaspoon vanilla extract
- 1/2 teaspoon baking soda
- 12-inch-long wooden skewer

### DECORATIONS

- 1 tube (4.25 ounces) white decorating icing
- 4 black jelly beans, cut in half and discarding one piece
- 1 candy corn
- 1 red fruit-flavored gumdrop, cut in half
- 1 1 1/4-inch-wide by 23-inch-long fleece piece for scarf
- 4 3-inch-wide by 3 1/2-inch-wide felt pieces for mittens
- Craft glue
- 2 small bows
- 2 5-inch-long wooden skewers
- 1 small hat

For once it's okay for kids to play with their food! As a party activity, set out bowls of popcorn and candy and let the children string holiday necklaces. A gingerbread cookie pendant decorated as a snowman face is sure to have everyone smiling.

# edible necklaces

Children will have fun creating edible cookie and candy necklaces! Use a needle and heavy-duty thread (adult supervision may be needed) to string popcorn, cellophane-wrapped peppermints, and candies with holes in the centers into a necklace. Use ribbon to tie a snowman face cookie to each necklace. The cookies were made using the Snowman Gingerbread Cookies recipe, page 87, and a 2-inch round cookie cutter. Before baking the cookies, candies for eyes, noses, and mouths were pressed into dough and a drinking straw was used to make a hole for the ribbon.

- Popped white popcorn
- Cellophane-wrapped peppermints
- Fruit-flavored candies with holes in the center
- 2-inch round gingerbread snowman cookie faces
- $1/16$-inch-wide ribbon
- Large-eyed needle
- Heavy-duty thread

Who can resist a sweetly decorated gingerbread cookie snowman? The cookies come alive when you add candy eyes, noses, and buttons. Tubes of decorating icing make it easy to pipe on each hat and scarf.

# snowman gingerbread cookies

In a large bowl, cream butter and brown sugar until fluffy. Add molasses and egg; beat until smooth. In a medium bowl, combine flour and next 6 ingredients; add to butter mixture and stir until a soft dough forms. Divide dough into 4 balls and wrap in plastic wrap; chill 2 hours.

On a lightly floured surface, roll out dough to ¼-inch thickness. Use a 4¾-inch-high snowman cookie cutter to cut out cookies. Place on a greased baking sheet. Press in candies for eyes, noses, and buttons. Bake in a preheated 350° oven for 7 to 9 minutes or until edges are firm. Transfer cookies to a wire rack to cool.

Pipe black icing for hats and white icing for scarves. Allow icing to harden.

**YIELD:** about 15

½ cup butter or margarine, softened

½ cup firmly packed brown sugar

½ cup molasses

1 egg

2½ cups all-purpose flour

2 teaspoons ground ginger

1 teaspoon ground cinnamon

1 teaspoon baking soda

½ teaspoon ground nutmeg

¼ teaspoon ground cloves

¼ teaspoon salt

Mini candy-coated chocolate candy

2 tubes (4.25 ounces each) black and white decorating icings and a set of decorating tips

Made with only three simple ingredients, Minty Marshmallow Fruit Dip is a sweet treat for dunking apple slices. Kids will love its little crunchy bits of peppermint candy.

# minty marshmallow fruit dip

In a medium bowl, beat cream cheese and marshmallow creme until fluffy. Stir in $1/4$ cup peppermint candies. Garnish, if desired. Serve with apple slices.

**YIELD:** about $1^3/4$ cups

1  **package (8 ounces) cream cheese, softened**

1  **jar (7 ounces) marshmallow creme**

$1/4$  **cup finely crushed peppermint candies**

**GARNISH: crushed peppermint candies**

**Apple slices to serve**

# HOLIDAY OPEN HOUSE

Good food. Good friends. Put them together and you've got a party, whether it's impromptu or the result of careful planning. The recipes for appetizers, drinks, and desserts in this collection represent a good assortment from which to choose. Keep it small or go large. There are tastes here to please everyone!

## recipes

Sausage Bundles

Hot Mulled Wine

Hot and Sweet Tidbits

Bacon-Cheese New Potatoes

Festive Cheese Ball

Tortellini Kabobs

Marinated Pork Tenderloin Sandwiches

Jezebel Sauce

Orange Glazed Pecans

Herb Marinated Shrimp

Party Meatballs

Saucy Sausages

Bacon-Cheddar Spread

Peppermint Crunch Candy

Triple Chip Cookies

Cheesecake Bites

Wreath Candy

Chocolate-Coconut Cream Fudge

Sparkling Fruit Tea

Praline Coffee

Merry Cherry Cocktails

**Shown on opposite page:**
Party guests love choices, such as these Sausage Bundles (left) and Bacon-Cheese New Potatoes. Hot and Sweet Tidbits (in container) are great for munching while sipping Hot Mulled Wine.

## party tips

• The number of guests expected and what you know about their food and drink preferences should guide your party menu. Small, intimate gatherings could succeed with a single drink offering, two appetizers, and one sweet treat. As the guest list grows and becomes more diverse, multiply the number of different beverages, appetizers, and sweets.

• Provide a balanced mix of foods that are savory or sweet, crunchy or moist, light or luscious. Likewise, offer drinks that are hot as well as cold, rich and creamy or clear and crisp, and spirited or nonalcoholic.

• Plan to use make-ahead dishes when possible so that you get to spend more time with your guests, and less in the kitchen. Fill out the menu with convenience foods such as chips and salsa; deli trays of meats, cheeses, and fresh vegetables; and bakery desserts.

• For take-home party favors, place a pretty basket of wrapped cookies or other treats near the door.

Hot and Sweet Tidbits

Sausage Bundles
Bacon-Cheese New Potatoes

Hot Mulled Wine

# sausage bundles

On a lightly floured surface, roll out each sheet of pastry to a 10-inch square. Spread mustard evenly over pastry. Sprinkle cheese evenly over mustard. Cut pastry into 2½-inch squares. Press each square into a miniature muffin pan. Spoon about 1 teaspoon sausage into each cup. Bring corners of pastry together and twist to seal. Bake in a preheated 350° oven for 10 to 12 minutes or until tops are lightly browned. Serve warm.

**YIELD:** about 2½ dozen

- 1 package (17¼ ounces) puff pastry, thawed
- 3 tablespoons Dijon-style mustard
- ¼ cup grated Parmesan cheese
- ½ pound mild pork sausage, cooked, crumbled, and drained well

# hot mulled wine

Combine wine and apple juice in a 1-gallon container. Tie spices in a small square of cheesecloth; add to wine mixture. Cover and chill overnight.

Remove spice bag and heat wine in a Dutch oven. Serve hot.

**YIELD:** about 4 quarts

- 2 quarts Burgundy or other dry red wine
- 2 quarts apple juice
- 3 cinnamon sticks (3 inches each)
- 1½ teaspoons whole cloves
- 1 teaspoon whole allspice

# hot and sweet tidbits

In a large greased roasting pan, combine cereals, popcorn, and nuts. In a medium saucepan, combine butter, corn syrup, cinnamon candies, sugar, chili powder, salt, and red pepper. Stirring constantly, bring to a boil over medium heat. Continue stirring until candies melt. Pour over cereal mixture; stir until well coated.

Bake at 250° for 1 hour, stirring every 15 minutes. Spread on aluminum foil to cool completely. Stir in chocolate pieces.

**YIELD:** about 34 cups

- 1 package (14 ounces) honey-nut round toasted oat cereal
- 1 package (12 ounces) square corn cereal
- 8 cups popped popcorn
- 1 can (11$\frac{1}{2}$ ounces) mixed nuts
- $\frac{1}{2}$ cup butter or margarine
- $\frac{1}{2}$ cup light corn syrup
- $\frac{1}{2}$ cup small red cinnamon candies
- $\frac{1}{2}$ cup sugar
- 1 tablespoon chili powder
- $\frac{1}{4}$ teaspoon salt
- $\frac{1}{4}$ teaspoon ground red pepper
- 1 package (16 ounces) red and green candy-coated chocolate pieces

# bacon-cheese new potatoes

Rub potatoes with oil and place on an ungreased baking sheet; bake at 375° for 35 to 45 minutes or until tender. Allow potatoes to cool enough to handle.

Cut potatoes in half. Cut a small slice from bottom of each potato half so potatoes will sit level. Using a small melon baller, scoop out a small portion of potato pulp, leaving at least a $\frac{1}{4}$-inch shell; reserve potato pulp.

In a medium bowl, beat potato pulp, Gruyère cheese, sour cream, green onions, cream cheese, basil, garlic, salt, and pepper with an electric mixer; stir in bacon. Spoon potato mixture into each potato shell; place on a greased baking sheet. Bake at 375° for 7 to 12 minutes or until lightly browned. Garnish, if desired. Serve warm.

**YIELD:** about 2 dozen

- 1$\frac{1}{2}$ pounds new potatoes
- 2 tablespoons olive oil
- 1 cup finely shredded Gruyère cheese
- $\frac{1}{2}$ cup sour cream
- $\frac{1}{2}$ cup minced green onions
- 3 ounces cream cheese, softened
- 2 tablespoons minced fresh basil or 1 teaspoon dried basil leaves
- 1 garlic clove, minced
- $\frac{1}{4}$ teaspoon salt
- $\frac{1}{4}$ teaspoon pepper
- 8 ounces bacon, cooked and crumbled

    **GARNISHES:** bacon and chopped green onion tops

Decorated to resemble a Christmas ornament, this Festive Cheese Ball is a tasty blend of Parmesan and cream cheeses. Bits of celery and carrots give each bite a touch of crunch, and cutouts of red, green, and yellow peppers transform the ball into a pretty table accent.

# festive cheese ball

In a medium bowl, combine Neufchâtel cheese, celery, Parmesan cheese, carrot, mayonnaise, and dried onion. On a serving plate, shape cheese mixture into a ball. Cover and refrigerate 8 hours or overnight to allow flavors to blend.

Garnish cheese ball with peppers cut with an aspic cutter or knife. Arrange a piece of yellow pepper and a folded piece of green onion top to resemble ornament hanger.

To serve, let stand at room temperature 20 to 30 minutes or until softened. Serve with crackers.

**YIELD:** 1 cheese ball

1 package (8 ounces) Neufchâtel cheese, softened

$1/2$ cup finely chopped celery

$1/3$ cup grated Parmesan cheese

$1/4$ cup grated carrot

2 tablespoons mayonnaise

2 tablespoons dried minced onion

GARNISHES: sweet red, green, and yellow peppers and green onion top

Crackers to serve

Tempt your guests with appetizing skewers of Tortellini Kabobs. Each has a flavor-packed assortment of cheese-filled tortellini, artichoke hearts, ripe olives, and pepperoni slices marinated in Italian dressing. Cheese cubes and cherry tomatoes top them off.

# tortellini kabobs

*Make ahead to allow enough time for kabobs to marinate.*

Prepare tortellini according to package directions; drain and cool. Place tortellini, artichoke hearts, olives, and pepperoni on skewers. Place skewers in a 9 x 13-inch baking dish; drizzle with salad dressing, turning skewers to coat. Cover and chill 8 hours, turning occasionally.

To serve, remove kabobs from dressing; add cheese cubes and tomato halves.

**YIELD:** about 4$^1$/$_2$ dozen

1 package (9 ounces) uncooked refrigerated cheese-filled tortellini

1 can (14 ounces) artichoke hearts, drained and quartered

1 can (6 ounces) pitted ripe olives, drained

1 package (3.5 ounces) pepperoni slices (about 1$^1$/$_2$-inch diameter)

6-inch-long wooden skewers

1 bottle (8 ounces) Italian salad dressing

8 ounces farmer cheese, cut into $^1$/$_2$-inch cubes

1 pint cherry tomatoes, halved

Little sandwiches of Marinated Pork Tenderloin spread with robust Jezebel Sauce will be the talk of the party. Grilled or baked, the seasoned meat can be served warm or cold alongside a dish of extra sauce, a kicky blend of apple jelly, marmalade, mustard, and horseradish.

# marinated pork tenderloin sandwiches

In a shallow dish or large heavy-duty resealable plastic bag, combine soy sauce, sherry, olive oil, dry mustard, ginger, sesame oil, hot sauce, and garlic; add tenderloins. Cover or seal and chill 8 hours, turning tenderloins occasionally.

Remove tenderloins from marinade, reserving $1/2$ cup marinade. In a saucepan, combine reserved marinade and apple cider vinegar; bring to a boil and boil 1 minute; set aside.

To cook tenderloins on a grill, cover with grill lid, turning occasionally and basting with marinade mixture during first 15 minutes of cooking time. Cook over medium-hot coals (350° to 400°) for 20 to 25 minutes or until a meat thermometer registers 160°. Remove tenderloins from heat; let stand 5 minutes. Slice and serve warm or chilled with rolls and Jezebel Sauce.

**YIELD:** 3 dozen

**NOTE:** Tenderloins may be baked at 375° for 25 to 35 minutes instead of grilled.

- $1/4$ cup lite soy sauce
- $1/4$ cup dry sherry or Madeira
- 2 tablespoons olive oil
- 1 tablespoon dry mustard
- 1 teaspoon ground ginger
- 1 teaspoon sesame oil
- 8 drops hot sauce
- 2 cloves garlic, minced
- 2 pork tenderloins ($3/4$ pound each)
- $1/2$ cup apple cider vinegar
- 3 dozen rolls
  Jezebel Sauce

# jezebel sauce

In a small bowl, beat apple jelly at medium speed of an electric mixer until smooth. Add marmalade, mustard, horseradish, and pepper; beat at medium speed until blended. Cover and chill.

**YIELD:** about 3 cups

- 1 cup apple jelly
- 1 cup pineapple-orange marmalade or pineapple preserves
- 1 jar (6 ounces) prepared mustard
- 1 jar (5 ounces) prepared horseradish
- $1/4$ teaspoon pepper

Orange Glazed Pecans are an irresistible offering. Guests will keep returning to the table for them along with bites of flavorful Herb Marinated Shrimp.

# orange glazed pecans

In a medium saucepan, combine sugars, sour cream, and orange juice. Stirring constantly, cook over medium-low heat until sugars dissolve. Using a pastry brush dipped in hot water, wash down any sugar crystals on sides of pan. Attach candy thermometer to pan, making sure thermometer does not touch bottom of pan.

Increase heat to medium and bring to a boil. Cook, without stirring, until syrup reaches soft-ball stage (approximately 234° to 240°). Test about $^1/_2$ teaspoon syrup in ice water. Syrup should easily form a ball in ice water but flatten when held in your hand. Remove from heat; stir in orange extract. Add pecans and stir until well coated. Spread pecan mixture on buttered aluminum foil. Allow to dry uncovered at room temperature 24 hours. Break apart and store in an airtight container.

**YIELD:** about $4^1/_4$ cups

$^1/_2$ cup granulated sugar

$^1/_2$ cup firmly packed brown sugar

$^1/_2$ cup sour cream

2 tablespoons frozen orange juice concentrate, thawed

1 teaspoon orange extract

3 cups unsalted pecan halves, toasted

# herb marinated shrimp

Bring water and lemon to a boil; add shrimp and cook 3 to 5 minutes or until shrimp turn pink. Drain well; rinse with cold water. Chill.

Peel and devein shrimp. Place shrimp in a large heavy-duty resealable plastic bag.

Combine vegetable oil, pepper sauce, garlic, olive oil, salt, seafood seasoning, basil, oregano, thyme, and parsley; stir well and pour over shrimp. Seal bag; marinate in refrigerator 8 hours.

Drain shrimp before serving.

**YIELD:** about 25 appetizer servings

3 quarts water

1 large lemon, sliced

4 pounds unpeeled large fresh shrimp

2 cups vegetable oil

$^1/_4$ cup hot pepper sauce

1 tablespoon minced garlic

1 tablespoon olive oil

$1^1/_2$ teaspoons salt

$1^1/_2$ teaspoons seafood seasoning

$1^1/_2$ teaspoons dried basil leaves

$1^1/_2$ teaspoons dried oregano leaves

$1^1/_2$ teaspoons dried thyme leaves

$1^1/_2$ teaspoons minced fresh parsley

Meat lovers will gravitate to big bowls of Party Meatballs and Saucy Sausages. The heavily seasoned meatballs bask in a rich sauce made of mustard, ketchup, and molasses. Plum jam and mustard coat the little smoked cocktail sausages.

# party meatballs

Process first 13 ingredients in a large food processor until blended. Add beef, stuffing mix, and flour; pulse until blended. Shape beef mixture into 32 balls.

In a large skillet, cook meatballs in batches in hot oil over medium-high heat 7 minutes or until done. (Gently shake pan over burner often to turn and brown meatballs evenly.) Transfer meatballs to a chafing dish or electric slow cooker and keep warm.

In a small saucepan, combine mustard, ketchup, and molasses. Cook over medium heat until sauce is warm. Pour sauce over meatballs and serve warm.

**YIELD:** 32 appetizers

1 small onion, quartered
1/3 cup water
1 large egg
1 tablespoon sugar
1 1/4 teaspoons salt
1 teaspoon dried marjoram leaves
1/2 teaspoon curry powder
1/4 teaspoon dried thyme leaves
1/4 teaspoon ground ginger
1/4 teaspoon ground cloves
1/4 teaspoon rubbed sage
Pinch of ground cinnamon
Pinch of ground nutmeg
1 pound ground beef
3/4 cup herb-seasoned stuffing mix
2 tablespoons all-purpose flour
1 tablespoon vegetable oil
1/2 cup prepared mustard
1/2 cup ketchup
1/2 cup molasses

# saucy sausages

In a large saucepan over medium-low heat, combine jam and mustard; stir until smooth. Add sausages; stirring occasionally, cook 10 to 15 minutes or until heated through. Serve warm.

**YIELD:** about 4 dozen

1 jar (18 ounces) red plum jam
1/4 cup prepared mustard
1 package (16 ounces) smoked cocktail sausages

O Christmas Tree, O Christmas Tree, how tasty are your branches! Bacon-Cheddar Spread will have guests singing its praises once they dip into the delicious mix of crumbled bacon, shredded cheese, chopped green onions, and toasted almonds.

# bacon-cheddar spread

Combine bacon, cheese, green onions, mayonnaise, almonds, and cayenne pepper in a medium bowl. Shape cheese mixture into a tree shape on serving plate. Refrigerate overnight.

Decorate with parsley, tomato, and bread pieces. Serve with crackers or party rye.

**YIELD:** 20 to 25 servings

1 package (12 ounces) bacon, cooked and crumbled

1 pound extra-sharp Cheddar cheese, shredded

1 bunch green onions, finely chopped

2 cups mayonnaise

1/2 cup toasted, slivered almonds

1 teaspoon cayenne pepper

Fresh parsley, cherry tomato, and rye bread pieces to decorate

Crackers or party rye to serve

Crushed peppermints give holiday color to Peppermint Crunch Candy, an easy treat that combines pieces of vanilla sandwich cookies with melted vanilla candy coating. Triple Chip Cookies include white chocolate and mint chips for a delicious twist on an old favorite.

# peppermint crunch candy

Place about 5¹/₂ dozen paper candy cups on baking sheets; set aside.

Melt candy coating in top of a double boiler over hot, not simmering, water. Fold cookie pieces into melted candy coating. Drop rounded teaspoonfuls of mixture into candy cups. Sprinkle crushed peppermint candy over tops before candy coating hardens. Chill about 15 minutes or until candy is firm.

Store in a cool place.

**YIELD:** about 5¹/₂ dozen

1 package (24 ounces) vanilla candy coating

26 vanilla sandwich cookies, coarsely chopped

Crushed peppermint candy

# triple chip cookies

Cream butter and sugars. Beat in eggs and vanilla. Combine flour, baking soda, baking powder, and salt; gradually add to creamed mixture. Stir in chips. Drop heaping teaspoonfuls of dough onto greased baking sheets. Bake in a preheated 350° oven for 10 to 12 minutes or just until bottoms are lightly browned. Do not overbake.

**YIELD:** about 6 dozen

1 cup butter or margarine, softened

1¹/₂ cups firmly packed light brown sugar

¹/₂ cup granulated sugar

2 eggs

2 teaspoons vanilla extract

2 cups all-purpose flour

1 teaspoon baking soda

¹/₂ teaspoon baking powder

¹/₂ teaspoon salt

1¹/₂ cups semisweet chocolate chips

1 cup mint chips

³/₄ cup white chocolate chips

Say "Happy Holidays" in a merry way with pecan-topped Cheesecake Bites and colorful Wreath Candy. Tinted cornflake cereal forms the leafy rings, which are adorned with red cinnamon candy "ornaments."

# cheesecake bites

Combine flour, pecans, and brown sugar in a medium bowl. Stir in melted butter until blended. Reserve 1/3 cup of mixture; press remainder into bottom of a greased 8-inch square baking pan. Bake in a preheated 350° oven for 12 to 15 minutes.

While crust is baking, beat cream cheese and granulated sugar until smooth. Beat in egg, milk, lemon juice, and vanilla. Pour over baked crust; sprinkle with reserved pecan mixture. Return to oven and bake at 350° for 25 minutes longer. Cool slightly; cut into 1 1/2-inch squares. Cool completely. Store in refrigerator.

**YIELD:** about 2 dozen

- 1 cup all-purpose flour
- 1/2 cup chopped pecans
- 1/3 cup firmly packed light brown sugar
- 1/3 cup butter or margarine, melted
- 1 package (8 ounces) cream cheese, softened
- 1/4 cup granulated sugar
- 1 egg
- 2 tablespoons milk
- 1 tablespoon lemon juice
- 1 teaspoon vanilla extract

# wreath candy

In a large saucepan, mix butter, corn syrup, sugar, and food coloring. Cook over medium heat until mixture boils, stirring constantly. Boil 5 minutes, stirring frequently; remove from heat. Add cereal and stir until well blended.

Drop mixture by buttered 1/4 cupfuls onto waxed paper. Use buttered fingers to shape each portion to resemble a wreath; decorate with cinnamon candies. Let stand until firm.

**YIELD:** about 1 dozen

- 3 tablespoons butter or margarine
- 1/2 cup light corn syrup
- 3 tablespoons sugar
- 3/4 teaspoon green liquid food coloring
- 3 1/2 cups cornflake cereal
  Small red cinnamon candies to decorate

Chocolate-Coconut Cream Fudge is the stuff that sweet dreams are made of! Chock full of rich flavor, the creamy confection will melt in their mouths. Individually wrapped squares also would make wonderful favors to send departing guests happily on their way.

# chocolate-coconut cream fudge

Line a 9-inch square baking pan with aluminum foil, extending foil over 2 sides of pan; grease foil and set aside.

Butter sides of a heavy large saucepan. Combine sugar, cream of coconut, evaporated milk, corn syrup, butter, and salt. Stirring constantly, cook over medium-low heat until sugar dissolves. Using a pastry brush dipped in hot water, wash down any sugar crystals on sides of pan. Attach a candy thermometer to pan, making sure thermometer does not touch bottom of pan.

Increase heat to medium and bring to a boil. Cook, without stirring, until mixture reaches soft-ball stage (approximately 234° to 240°). Test about $1/2$ teaspoon mixture in ice water. Mixture will easily form a ball in ice water but will flatten when removed from water. Place pan in 2 inches of cold water in sink. Add vanilla; do not stir. Cool to approximately 110°. Remove from sink. Stir in chocolate chips. Using medium speed of an electric mixer, beat until fudge thickens and begins to lose its gloss. Pour into prepared pan. Chill 1 hour or until firm.

Use ends of foil to lift fudge from pan. Cut into 1-inch squares. Store in refrigerator.

**YIELD:** about 5 dozen pieces

$2^1/_4$ cups sugar

1 can ($8^1/_2$ ounces) cream of coconut

1 cup evaporated milk

2 tablespoons light corn syrup

1 tablespoon butter or margarine

$1/_8$ teaspoon salt

1 teaspoon vanilla extract

1 package (6 ounces) semisweet chocolate chips

Quench their thirst for flavor with these delicious drinks. Sparkling Fruit Tea features apple and white grape juices. Spirited Praline Coffee is enriched with vanilla ice cream. Merry Cherry Cocktails are a frothy combination laced with rum and cherry brandy.

# sparkling fruit tea

In a large saucepan, bring 4 cups water to a boil. Remove from heat; add tea bags. Cover and steep 10 minutes; remove tea bags. Add sugar; stir until dissolved. In a 1-gallon container, combine apple juice concentrate and cold water. Stir in tea mixture. Cover and chill.

To serve, add grape juice to tea mixture. Serve immediately over ice.

YIELD: about 13 cups

- 4 cups water
- 15 orange and spice-flavored tea bags
- 1 cup sugar
- 1 can (12 ounces) frozen apple juice concentrate, thawed
- $4\frac{1}{2}$ cups cold water
- 1 bottle (750 ml) sparkling white grape juice, chilled

# praline coffee

In a Dutch oven, combine coffee, milk, and sugar. Stirring occasionally, cook over medium-high heat until mixture begins to boil; remove from heat. Stir in ice cream, vodka, vanilla, and maple flavoring. Serve hot.

YIELD: about twenty 6-ounce servings

- 2 quarts brewed coffee
- 3 cans (12 ounces each) evaporated skim milk
- $\frac{1}{2}$ cup firmly packed brown sugar
- 3 cups fat-free vanilla ice cream, softened
- 1 cup vodka
- 1 tablespoon vanilla extract
- 2 teaspoons maple flavoring

# merry cherry cocktails

Place half and half, cream of coconut, dark rum, cherry brandy, cherry juice, and grenadine in a blender and mix well. Add ice and blend until frothy. Pour into cups; garnish, if desired.

YIELD: 5 to 6 servings

- $\frac{2}{3}$ cup half and half
- $\frac{1}{2}$ cup cream of coconut
- $\frac{1}{3}$ cup dark rum
- $\frac{1}{3}$ cup cherry brandy
- 3 tablespoons maraschino cherry juice
- 3 teaspoons grenadine
- $1\frac{1}{2}$ to 2 cups ice cubes
- GARNISHES: whipped cream and maraschino cherries

# NEW YEAR'S BRUNCH

Welcome the New Year with a relaxing brunch that celebrates the pleasures of good food enjoyed with family and friends. This versatile menu accommodates diners who prefer a large morning meal, as well as light eaters who simply want a bagel or sweet roll. For prosperity in the coming year, consider adding some traditional "good luck" foods—and leave a little on your plate to guarantee that you'll have plenty to eat all year!

## recipes

**Crab-Cream Cheese Bake**
**Brunch Eggs**
**Sunrise Mimosas**
**Shrimp Rémoulade**
**Overnight Fruit Salad**
**Creamy Orange Bagel Spread**
**Cranberry-Pear Rolls**

**Shown on opposite page:**
Crab-Cream Cheese Bake is so delicious that no one will guess the flaky pastry is made from refrigerated crescent roll dough. Brunch Eggs casserole features a flavorful Cheddar cheese sauce. Sunrise Mimosas are an eye-opening blend of orange and cranberry juices.

## party tips

• This combination breakfast-lunch is a pleasant way to start the first day of the year. Scheduling the brunch to begin at 10 or 11 a.m. will be appreciated by any guests who had a late night of New Year's Eve partying.

• Set a cheery table that will counter winter's typical grey skies and foster a mood of optimism.

• To keep the eggs and other foods warm throughout the brunch, serve them in chafing dishes.

• There are a number of popular New Year's traditions for attracting good luck in the coming year. During the meal, invite everyone to talk about their favorite traditions or to share their New Year's resolutions.

Crab-Cream Cheese Bake

Brunch Eggs

Sunrise Mimosas

# crab-cream cheese bake

In a medium bowl, combine cream cheese, onions, and dill weed. Unroll crescent roll dough onto a greased baking sheet, being careful not to separate dough into pieces. Press dough into an 8 x 11-inch rectangle.

Spoon crabmeat lengthwise along center of dough. Spoon cream cheese mixture over crabmeat. Fold long edges of dough over cream cheese mixture, slightly overlapping edges; pinch edges together to seal.

Place, seam side down, on baking sheet. Lightly brush top of dough with egg yolk. Cut slits in top of dough. Bake in a preheated 350° oven for 20 to 22 minutes or until golden brown and flaky. Cut into 1-inch slices and serve warm.

**YIELD:** about 12 servings

- 1 package (8 ounces) cream cheese, softened
- ¼ cup chopped green onions
- ½ teaspoon dried dill weed
- 1 can (8 ounces) refrigerated crescent rolls
- 1 can (6½ ounces) crabmeat, drained
- 1 egg yolk, beaten

# brunch eggs

In a saucepan, melt ¼ cup butter. Stir in 1 cup onions and sauté until soft. Whisk in flour and, whisking slowly, cook over medium heat for 2 minutes. Gradually whisk in milk and cook until thickened. Whisk in cheese, sherry, seasoned salt, dry mustard, curry powder, white pepper, and cayenne pepper; cook until cheese melts. Cool.

Beat eggs with water. Scramble eggs in remaining ¼ cup butter and oil until barely set. Salt and pepper to taste.

Butter two 2-quart casseroles. Pour a small amount of cheese sauce into bottom of each casserole. Spoon scrambled eggs evenly into casseroles and cover with remainder of sauce. If the casseroles are being made in advance, cover tightly and refrigerate until ready to bake. (It is important that eggs be completely covered with sauce.)

When ready to serve, bring casseroles to room temperature and bake, covered, at 275° for 1 hour. (Eggs may be kept warm over hot water until ready to serve.) Sprinkle with remaining ½ cup green onions. Serve warm.

**YIELD:** about 12 servings

- ½ cup butter, divided
- 1½ cups green onions, chopped including tops and divided
- ¼ cup all-purpose flour
- 2½ cups milk
- 1 cup (4 ounces) shredded sharp Cheddar cheese
- ¼ cup sherry
- ¾ teaspoon seasoned salt
- ½ teaspoon dry mustard
- ¼ teaspoon curry powder
- ¼ teaspoon ground white pepper
- ¼ teaspoon cayenne pepper
- 18 eggs
- 1 cup water
- 2 tablespoons vegetable oil
  Salt and pepper

# sunrise mimosas

Pour vodka, cranberry juice, and orange juice into a pitcher and mix. Chill or pour over ice cubes. Garnish, if desired.

**YIELD:** 5 to 6 servings

- ¾ cup vodka
- 2½ cups cranberry juice
- 1½ cups orange juice
  **GARNISH:** orange slices

Shrimp Rémoulade is cool and refreshing, featuring chilled shrimp and fresh sweet pepper strips on a bed of Romaine lettuce. The zippy Creole sauce is prepared ahead so the flavors can blend overnight.

# shrimp rémoulade

In a medium bowl, combine mayonnaise, green onions, celery, parsley, Creole mustard, lemon juice, pickles, capers, garlic, paprika, horseradish, anchovy paste, and tarragon; stir until well blended. Cover and chill overnight.

To serve, spoon rémoulade sauce into a small bowl and place on a large serving plate. Place lettuce around bowl. Arrange shrimp and pepper slices on lettuce.

YIELD: 8 servings

2 cups mayonnaise

1 cup finely chopped green onions

½ cup finely chopped celery

¼ cup chopped fresh parsley

2 tablespoons Creole mustard

1 tablespoon freshly squeezed lemon juice

1 tablespoon finely chopped sour pickles

1 tablespoon drained capers

2 garlic cloves, minced

1 teaspoon paprika

1 teaspoon prepared horseradish

1 teaspoon anchovy paste

½ teaspoon finely chopped fresh tarragon leaves

Romaine lettuce, torn

1¼ pounds medium shrimp, cooked, shelled (leaving tails on), deveined, and chilled

1 sweet red pepper, cut into strips with a crinkle-cut garnishing tool

1 green pepper, cut into strips with a crinkle-cut garnishing tool

Wake up your taste buds with a simple bagel topped with *Creamy Orange Bagel Spread*. For a richer meal, indulge in *Overnight Fruit Salad*, a sweet and tangy combination of pineapple chunks, cherries, mandarin oranges, and miniature marshmallows in a creamy dressing.

# overnight fruit salad

Chill a small bowl and beaters from an electric mixer in freezer. Place pineapple chunks in a large bowl; set aside.

In the top of a double boiler over hot water, combine egg yolks, sugar, vinegar, reserved pineapple syrup, butter, and salt. Stirring constantly, cook mixture about 4 minutes or until thickened. Remove from heat and allow to cool; chill 30 minutes.

Add cherries, mandarin oranges, and marshmallows to pineapple chunks. Stir in chilled dressing. In chilled bowl, beat whipping cream until stiff peaks form; fold into fruit mixture. Chill fruit salad overnight.

**YIELD:** about 16 servings

1 can (20 ounces) pineapple chunks in heavy syrup, drained and reserving 2 tablespoons syrup

3 egg yolks, beaten

2 tablespoons sugar

2 tablespoons white vinegar

1 tablespoon butter or margarine

$1/8$ teaspoon salt

2 cans (17 ounces each) pitted white Royal Anne cherries, drained

2 cans (11 ounces each) mandarin oranges, drained

$1^1/2$ cups miniature marshmallows

1 cup whipping cream

# creamy orange bagel spread

In a medium bowl, beat cream cheese until fluffy. Add orange juice and orange extract. Gradually beat in confectioners sugar. Serve with bagels.

**YIELD:** about $1^1/3$ cups

1 package (8 ounces) cream cheese, softened

$1^1/2$ tablespoons orange juice

$1/2$ teaspoon orange extract

$3/4$ cup confectioners sugar

Bagels to serve

Apple pie spice really brings out the flavor of the chopped pears and dried cranberries in these moist rolls. The confectioners sugar glaze makes the tender pastries even more irresistible.

# cranberry-pear rolls

For rolls, combine sugar and water in a heavy medium saucepan over medium-high heat. Stirring frequently, bring to a boil and cook until sugar dissolves; set aside to cool.

Pour melted butter evenly into two 8-inch square baking pans. In a medium bowl, combine flour, baking powder, and salt. Using a pastry blender or 2 knives, cut shortening into dry ingredients until mixture resembles coarse meal. Add milk, egg, and vanilla; stir just until moistened.

On a lightly floured surface, roll out dough to a 10 x 18-inch rectangle. Sprinkle pears and cranberries over dough to within 1 inch of edges. Sprinkle apple pie spice over fruit. Beginning at 1 long edge, carefully roll up dough jellyroll style. Pinch seam to seal. Cut roll into 1-inch slices. Place in pans with cut side down and sides touching. Pour syrup over dough. Bake in a preheated 350° oven for 50 to 60 minutes or until golden brown.

For glaze, combine confectioners sugar, water, and vanilla in a small bowl; stir until smooth. Drizzle over warm rolls. Serve warm or cool completely.

**YIELD:** 2 pans rolls, about 9 rolls in each pan

**ROLLS**

- 2 cups sugar
- 2 cups water
- $1/2$ cup butter or margarine, melted
- $2^1/2$ cups all-purpose flour
- $2^3/4$ teaspoons baking powder
- $1/2$ teaspoon salt
- $3/4$ cup vegetable shortening
- $1/2$ cup milk
- 1 egg, beaten
- $1^1/2$ teaspoons vanilla extract
- 3 cups finely chopped ripe pears (about 3 large pears)
- 1 package (6 ounces) sweetened dried cranberries, chopped
- $1^1/4$ teaspoons apple pie spice

**GLAZE**

- 1 cup confectioners sugar
- 3 to 4 teaspoons water
- 1 teaspoon vanilla extract

# CHOCOLATE INDULGENCE

Especially for Valentine's Day or any occasion celebrating love and romance, a party devoted to chocolate is right on target. Then again, any time is the right time for chocolate! Passions run deep for this dark, sweet temptation in all its many forms, from candy and cookies to cakes and pies. Indulge your guests with our dreamy selections—they'll love you for it!

## recipes

**Imperial Champagne Cocktails**
**Chocolate Shortbread**
**Chewy Chocolate Bars**
**Tunnel Cake**
**Chocolate-Mint Torte**
**Double Chocolate Cheesecake**
**Chocolate Fondue**
**White Chocolate Fondue**
**Chocolate Toffee Mud Pie**
**Almond Cappuccino**

**Shown on opposite page:**
A buffet arrangement allows party guests to fill their plates with the treats they find most irresistible, such as Tunnel Cake, Chocolate Shortbread hearts, and Chewy Chocolate Bars. Imperial Champagne Cocktails are an elegant beverage choice.

## party tips

• Chocolate parties can be tailored to different age groups. For adults, offer rich flavors and spirited drinks that will invite guests to luxuriate in the moment. For teens, how about a dress-up date night featuring trendy fondue and cheesecake? And don't forget the younger crowd—they'll think it's awesome to get hot cocoa and cookies!

• For a family gathering with mixed ages, set up separate areas offering treats for the different groups.

• Let the party be a chocolate swap. Ask everyone to bring their very favorite chocolate treat. Then after plenty of munching, encourage each guest to pack up a sampling of all the leftover goodies to take home. Some cooks might even be persuaded to share copies of their recipes.

• If you want to include a few non-sweet foods, check out the recipes in our Holiday Open House and other chapters.

Imperial Champagne Cocktails

Tunnel Cake
Chocolate Shortbread

Chewy Chocolate Bars

# imperial champagne cocktails

In a 2$\frac{1}{2}$-quart container, combine fruit punch, orange juice, and schnapps. Cover and refrigerate until well chilled.

To serve, stir in champagne. Serve chilled.

**YIELD:** about ten 6-ounce servings

**NOTE:** For a non-alcohol drink, use sparkling white grape juice instead of champagne and more orange juice for the schnapps.

2  **cups tropical fruit punch drink**

2  **cups orange juice**

1  **cup peach schnapps**

1  **bottle (750 ml) champagne, chilled**

# chocolate shortbread

In a large bowl, cream butter, confectioners sugar, and vanilla until fluffy. In a small bowl, combine flour, cocoa, and salt. Add flour mixture to creamed mixture; stir until well blended. Wrap dough in plastic wrap and chill 30 minutes.

Press dough into a 10$\frac{1}{2}$ x 15$\frac{1}{2}$-inch jellyroll pan. Bake in a preheated 300° oven for 30 minutes. Use a 2-inch-wide heart-shaped cookie cutter to cut out warm shortbread. Transfer cookies to a wire rack with waxed paper underneath to cool.

Sift confectioners sugar over cooled cookies.

**YIELD:** about 2 dozen

- 1 cup butter, softened
- $\frac{2}{3}$ cup confectioners sugar
- 1 teaspoon vanilla extract
- 1$\frac{1}{2}$ cups all-purpose flour
- $\frac{1}{4}$ cup cocoa
- $\frac{1}{4}$ teaspoon salt
  Confectioners sugar

# chewy chocolate bars

For crust, combine oats, corn syrup, brown sugar, melted butter, peanut butter, and vanilla in a medium bowl. Press mixture into a lightly greased 9 x 13-inch baking pan. Bake at 350° for 12 to 15 minutes; cool in pan.

For topping, melt chocolate chips and peanut butter in top of a double boiler over hot, not simmering, water. Stir in peanuts. Spread topping over crust. Cut into bars. Cover and chill until chocolate is firm. Store in refrigerator.

**YIELD:** about 4 dozen

**CRUST**

- 4 cups old-fashioned oats
- $\frac{3}{4}$ cup dark corn syrup
- 1 cup firmly packed brown sugar
- $\frac{2}{3}$ cup butter or margarine, melted
- $\frac{1}{2}$ cup crunchy peanut butter
- 2 teaspoons vanilla extract

**TOPPING**

- 1 package (12 ounces) semisweet chocolate chips
- $\frac{2}{3}$ cup crunchy peanut butter
- 1 cup coarsely chopped peanuts

This generously iced chocolate Tunnel Cake has a double surprise inside!
The creamy-delicious filling is loaded with miniature chocolate chips
(see page 125 for a peek).

# tunnel cake

For filling, combine cream cheese, sugar, and egg in a small bowl; beat until well blended. Stir in chocolate chips; set aside.

For cake, combine flour, sugar, cocoa, baking soda, and salt in a large bowl. Add water, oil, vinegar, and vanilla; beat until well blended. Pour half of batter into a well-greased 10-inch fluted tube pan. Spread filling over batter; top with remaining batter. Bake in a preheated 350° oven for 50 to 55 minutes or until toothpick inserted in center of cake comes out clean. Cool in pan 10 minutes. Invert cake onto a wire rack; cool completely.

For glaze, combine confectioners sugar, whipping cream, and vanilla. Drizzle over cake. Allow glaze to harden.

**YIELD:** about 16 servings

## FILLING

- 11 ounces cream cheese, softened
- $1/3$ cup sugar
- 1 egg
- 1 cup semisweet chocolate mini chips

## CAKE

- 3 cups all-purpose flour
- 2 cups sugar
- $1/2$ cup cocoa
- 2 teaspoons baking soda
- 1 teaspoon salt
- 2 cups water
- $2/3$ cup vegetable oil
- 2 tablespoons white vinegar
- 1 tablespoon vanilla extract

## GLAZE

- $1^3/4$ cups confectioners sugar
- 5 tablespoons whipping cream
- 1 teaspoon vanilla extract

One. Two. Three. This elegant Chocolate-Mint Torte is a triple delight! Its three layers of buttermilk chocolate cake are assembled with a rich crème de menthe filling. Shavings of chocolate dinner mints make an exquisite topping.

# chocolate-mint torte

Line bottoms of 3 ungreased 9-inch round cake pans with waxed paper; set aside.

For cake, cream butter and sugar in a large bowl until fluffy. Add eggs and vanilla; stir until smooth. Combine flour, baking powder, baking soda, and salt in a medium bowl. Alternately add buttermilk, liqueur, and dry ingredients to creamed mixture; beat until well blended. Stir in melted chocolate. Divide batter evenly into prepared pans. Bake in a preheated 350° oven for 20 to 25 minutes or until a toothpick inserted in center of cake comes out clean. Cool in pans 10 minutes; remove from pans and cool completely on a wire rack.

For filling, chill a small bowl and beaters from an electric mixer in freezer. In top of a double boiler over simmering water, combine egg whites, sugar, water, cream of tartar, and salt. Whisking constantly, cook until mixture reaches 160° on a candy thermometer (about 8 minutes). Transfer to a large bowl and beat until stiff peaks form. Gently fold melted chocolate into cooked mixture. In chilled bowl, beat whipping cream and crème de menthe until stiff peaks form. Gently fold into chocolate mixture. Refrigerate until ready to use.

To assemble cake, place 1 cake layer on a serving plate; spread one-third of filling on cake layer. Repeat with remaining layers and filling.

To garnish, use a vegetable peeler to shave chocolate mints; place on top of cake. Store in refrigerator.

YIELD: about 12 servings

## CAKE

- 1/2 cup butter or margarine, softened
- 1 3/4 cups sugar
- 2 eggs
- 1 teaspoon vanilla extract
- 2 cups all-purpose flour
- 1 teaspoon baking powder
- 1 teaspoon baking soda
- 1/4 teaspoon salt
- 3/4 cup buttermilk
- 1/2 cup coffee-flavored liqueur
- 4 ounces unsweetened baking chocolate, melted

## FILLING

- 4 egg whites
- 1/2 cup sugar
- 1 tablespoon water
- 1/4 teaspoon cream of tartar
- 1/8 teaspoon salt
- 8 ounces semisweet baking chocolate, melted
- 1 cup whipping cream
- 2 tablespoons crème de menthe

GARNISH: 15 individually wrapped chocolate wafer mints

Guests will be enamored with the rich Amaretto flavoring of Double Chocolate Cheesecake. The liqueur is in both the creamy chocolate cake and the dark chocolate glaze. The brown sugar-oatmeal crust has a touch of cinnamon and chopped almonds.

# double chocolate cheesecake

For oatmeal crust, process oats, almonds, brown sugar, butter, and cinnamon in a food processor until well blended. Press mixture into bottom of one 9-inch springform pan (mixture should be crumbly, but will hold together when pressed into pan). Bake in a preheated 350° oven for 6 to 8 minutes. Cool on a wire rack.

For chocolate cheese filling, beat cream cheese, sugar, and Amaretto in a large bowl until well blended. Add eggs, 1 at a time, beating well after each addition. Add melted chocolate; stir until mixture is thick and smooth. Spoon into baked crust. Bake in a preheated 350° oven for 30 to 35 minutes or until center is firm. Cool on a wire rack.

For chocolate glaze, melt chocolate and butter in a heavy small saucepan over low heat; stir until smooth. Remove pan from heat; stir in whipping cream and Amaretto. Spread glaze over cooled cheesecake. Chill several hours before serving.

For decorations, beat whipping cream until soft peaks form. Add confectioners sugar and vanilla; beat until stiff peaks form. Spoon mixture into a pastry bag fitted with a medium star tip. Pipe around bottom edge of cake and in center; insert almonds.

**YIELD:** 8 to 10 servings

## OATMEAL CRUST

- 1 cup quick-cooking oats
- 1/3 cup chopped almonds
- 1/3 cup firmly packed light brown sugar
- 1/4 cup butter, softened
- 1/2 teaspoon ground cinnamon

## CHOCOLATE CHEESE FILLING

- 2 packages (8 ounces each) cream cheese
- 1/2 cup sugar
- 1/4 cup Amaretto
- 4 eggs
- 4 ounces semisweet baking chocolate, melted

## CHOCOLATE GLAZE

- 4 ounces sweet dark baking chocolate, broken into pieces
- 1 tablespoon butter
- 3 tablespoons whipping cream
- 1/4 teaspoon Amaretto

## DECORATIONS

- 1 cup whipping cream
- 2 tablespoons confectioners sugar
- 1/2 teaspoon vanilla extract
- 1 tablespoon sliced almonds, toasted

*Luscious fruits and chunks of cake are lovely and delicious to serve with fondue. Offer both dark and white chocolate versions.*

# chocolate fondue

In a heavy medium saucepan, combine corn syrup and whipping cream. Bring mixture to a boil over medium heat. Remove from heat and add chocolate; stir until chocolate melts. Serve warm. Store in refrigerator.

To reheat, place sauce in a medium microwave-safe bowl and microwave on medium-high power (80%) 2 minutes or until chocolate softens; stir until smooth. Serve warm.

**YIELD:** about 1$^1$/$_2$ cups

1/2 cup light corn syrup

1/2 cup whipping cream

1 package (6 ounces) bittersweet baking chocolate, chopped

**SERVING OPTIONS: fresh or dried fruit, squares of angel food or pound cake, and other bite-size foods**

# white chocolate fondue

In a heavy large saucepan, combine whipping cream and sugar over medium heat. Stirring frequently, bring mixture to a boil. Reduce heat to medium low and simmer about 25 minutes or until liquid has been reduced to 2 cups. Remove from heat. Stir in crème de cacao and vanilla. Add white chocolate; stir until melted. Serve warm. Store in refrigerator.

To reheat, microwave sauce on medium power (50%) 8 minutes or until smooth, stirring after each minute. Serve warm.

**YIELD:** about 3 cups

3 cups whipping cream

1/2 cup sugar

1/4 cup white crème de cacao

1 1/2 teaspoons vanilla extract

12 ounces white chocolate, chopped

**SERVING OPTIONS: fresh or dried fruit, squares of angel food or pound cake, and other bite-size foods**

Chocolate Toffee Mud Pie is a mouth-watering combination of coffee ice cream, chocolate-covered toffee bars, and fudge sauce in a chocolate sandwich cookie crust. A cup of steamy Almond Cappuccino is a perfect partner.

# chocolate toffee mud pie

In a medium bowl, combine ice cream and 1 cup toffee pieces. Spoon into crust. Cover and freeze about 3 hours or until firm.

To serve, place fudge topping in a small microwave-safe bowl and microwave on high power (100%) 1 minute or until topping slightly melts. Stir in liqueur. Drizzle mixture over each serving and garnish with remaining chocolate-covered toffee pieces.

**YIELD:** about 8 servings

1 quart coffee-flavored ice cream, softened

5 bars (1.4 ounces each) chocolate-covered toffee, broken into bite-size pieces and divided

1 purchased chocolate pie crust (6 ounces)

1 container (12 ounces) fudge ice cream topping

2 tablespoons coffee-flavored liqueur

# almond cappuccino

In a large saucepan or Dutch oven, combine coffee, milk, and sugar. Stirring occasionally, cook over medium-high heat until mixture begins to boil; remove from heat. Stir in extracts. Serve hot.

**YIELD:** about sixteen 6-ounce servings

2 quarts brewed coffee

1 quart evaporated skim milk

$1/2$ cup firmly packed brown sugar

1 tablespoon vanilla extract

1 teaspoon almond extract

# KITCHEN TIPS

NOTE: For additional tips, see Success With Parties on page 7.

## MEASURING INGREDIENTS

Liquid measuring cups have a rim above the measuring line to keep liquid ingredients from spilling. Nested measuring cups are used to measure dry ingredients, butter, shortening, and peanut butter. Measuring spoons are used for measuring both dry and liquid ingredients.

**To measure flour or granulated sugar:** Spoon ingredient into nested measuring cup and level off with a knife. Do not pack down with spoon.

**To measure confectioners sugar:** Sift sugar, spoon lightly into nested measuring cup, and level off with a knife.

**To measure brown sugar:** Pack sugar into nested measuring cup and level off with a knife. Sugar should hold its shape when removed from cup.

**To measure butter, shortening, or peanut butter:** Pack ingredient firmly into nested measuring cup and level off with a knife.

**To measure liquids:** Use a liquid measuring cup placed on a flat surface. Pour ingredient into cup and check measuring line at eye level.

**To measure honey or syrup:** For a more accurate measurement, lightly spray measuring cup or spoon with cooking spray before measuring so the liquid will release easily from cup or spoon.

## SOFTENING BUTTER OR MARGARINE

To soften butter, remove wrapper from butter and place on a microwave-safe plate. Microwave 1 stick 20 to 30 seconds at medium-low power (30%).

## SOFTENING CREAM CHEESE

To soften cream cheese, remove wrapper from cream cheese and place on a microwave-safe plate. Microwave 1 to $1^1/_2$ minutes at medium power (50%) for an 8-ounce package or 30 to 45 seconds for a 3-ounce package.

## WHIPPING CREAM

For greatest volume, chill a glass bowl, beaters, and cream until well chilled before whipping. In warm weather, place chilled bowl over ice while whipping cream.

## TOASTING NUTS

Nuts will stay crisp better and have fuller flavor if toasted before combining with other ingredients. To toast nuts, spread nuts on an ungreased baking sheet. Stirring occasionally, bake 8 to 10 minutes in a preheated 350° oven until nuts are slightly darker in color. Watch carefully to prevent overcooking.

## PREPARING CITRUS FRUIT ZEST

To remove outer portion of peel (colored part) from citrus fruits, use a fine grater or fruit zester, being careful not to cut into the bitter white portion. Zest is also referred to as grated peel.

## BEATING EGG WHITES

For greatest volume, beat egg whites at room temperature in a clean, dry metal or glass bowl.

## MAKING CRUMBS

To make cookie or graham cracker crumbs, place crumbled pieces in a food processor or blender and pulse until finely ground. Or place pieces in a heavy-duty resealable plastic food storage bag and crush with a rolling pin.

## COOKING/OVEN TEMPERATURES

Our recipes indicate degrees Fahrenheit. For Celsius, see the Metric Equivalents table on page 142.

## CRITICAL TIMING

Because timing can be critical in some recipes (such as in candy-making), use a timer that counts seconds. Then you can anticipate when a minute is about to elapse.

## EGGS

Recipes were tested using large eggs.

## BUTTER

Recipes were tested using salted butter, unless otherwise specified in recipe.

- When butter is specified in a candy recipe, do not substitute light butter or margarine. Especially in chocolate recipes, the water content could cause problems.

## CHILLING DOUGH

To speed up chilling of dough, place in freezer about 20 minutes for each hour of chilling time indicated in recipe. If dough is to be rolled out into a rectangle or circle, shaping it into that form before chilling will make rolling out the dough much easier.

## CUTTING OUT COOKIES

Place a piece of white paper over pattern (for a more durable pattern, use acetate, a thin plastic used for stenciling that is available at craft stores). Use a permanent felt-tip pen with fine point to trace pattern; cut out pattern. Place pattern on rolled-out dough and use a small sharp knife to cut out cookies. (**Note:** If dough is sticky, dip knife frequently into flour while cutting out cookies.)

## BAKING TIPS

- Make sure to use fresh baking powder, baking soda, and self-rising flour.
- For flaky doughs, keep butter cold until you are ready to cut it into the dry ingredients.
- For lighter and fluffier breads and biscuits, don't overmix the dough.
- When rolling pie crust, sprinkle the work surface and the dough with flour frequently (but sparingly) to prevent sticking; too much extra flour could make the dough tough.
- To keep dough from sticking to cookie cutters, dip in flour before cutting out each cookie. Metal cookie cutters with a good edge usually will cut better than plastic cutters.
- Use heavy-gauge, shiny aluminum baking sheets with low or no sides for even browning of cookies. Dark coating on sheets will affect browning. Insulated sheets may make it more difficult to determine doneness; also, cookies with a high butter content will spread out before the shape is set.
- When recipe says to grease baking sheets, use a thin coating of vegetable shortening.
- When recipe says to line a pan with foil or waxed paper, grease pan first to help keep foil or waxed paper in place. Then grease foil or waxed paper if stated in recipe.
- Using parchment paper eliminates the need to grease cookie sheets and makes cleanup easy.
- Use recipe instructions to test for doneness. Since oven temperatures may vary, always check foods 1 minute before the earliest time stated in recipe to prevent overbaking.

## TESTS FOR CANDY MAKING

To determine the correct temperature of cooked candy, use a candy thermometer and the cold water test. Before each use, check the accuracy of your candy thermometer by attaching it to the side of a small saucepan of water, making sure thermometer does not touch bottom of pan. Bring water to a boil. Thermometer should register 212 degrees when water begins to boil. If it does not, adjust the temperature range for each candy consistency accordingly.

When using a candy thermometer, insert thermometer into candy mixture, making sure thermometer does not touch bottom of pan. Read temperature at eye level. Cook candy to desired temperature range. Working quickly, drop about 1/2 teaspoon of candy mixture into a cup of ice water. Use a fresh cup of water for each test. Use the following descriptions to determine if candy has reached the correct consistency:

Soft-Ball Stage (234 to 240 degrees): Candy will easily form a ball in ice water but will flatten when held in your hand.

Firm-Ball Stage (242 to 248 degrees): Candy will form a firm ball in ice water but will flatten if pressed when removed from the water.

Hard-Ball Stage (250 to 268 degrees): Candy will form a hard ball in ice water and will remain hard when removed from the water.

Soft-Crack Stage (270 to 290 degrees): Candy will form hard threads in ice water but will soften when removed from the water.

Hard-Crack Stage (300 to 310 degrees): Candy will form brittle threads in ice water and will remain brittle when removed from the water.

## MELTING CANDY COATING

Candy coating, also known as almond bark or chocolate bark, is often preferred over chocolate because it melts easily and isn't soft or tacky at room temperature.

To melt candy coating, place chopped coating in top of a double boiler over hot, not boiling, water or in a heavy saucepan over low heat. Stir occasionally with a dry spoon until coating melts. Remove from heat and use as desired.

To flavor candy coating, add a small amount of flavored oil.

To thin, add a small amount of vegetable oil, but no water.

If necessary, coating may be returned to heat to remelt. A way to keep coating warm for dipping candy is to place the pan of melted coating in a larger pan of hot water or in an electric skillet filled with water kept at the "Warm" setting.

## USING CHOCOLATE

Chocolate is best stored in a cool, dry place. Since it has a high content of cocoa butter, chocolate may develop a grey film, or "bloom," when temperatures change. This grey film does not affect the taste. When melting chocolate, a low temperature is important to prevent overheating and scorching that will affect flavor and texture. The following are methods for melting chocolate:

• Chocolate can be melted in a heavy saucepan over low heat, stirring constantly until melted.

• Melting chocolate in a double boiler over hot, not boiling, water is a good method to prevent chocolate from overheating.

• Using a microwave to melt chocolate is fast and convenient. To microwave chocolate, place in a microwave-safe container and microwave on medium-high power (80%) 1 minute; stir with a dry spoon. Continue to microwave 15 seconds at a time, stirring chocolate after each interval until smooth. Frequent stirring is important, as the chocolate will appear not to be melting, but will be soft when stirred. A shiny appearance is another sign that chocolate is melting.

## MAKING CHOCOLATE CURLS

Making chocolate curls for garnishes is not difficult, but it does take a little practice. The chocolate should be the correct firmness to form the curls, neither too soft nor too hard. Different types of baking chocolates may be used, but the most common ones are semisweet and unsweetened. They are usually packaged in boxes containing 1-ounce squares. There are several methods for making chocolate curls.

To make small, short curls, hold a baking chocolate square in your hand for a few minutes to slightly soften chocolate. Rub chocolate over shredding side (large holes) of a grater to form curls.

For medium-size curls, use a vegetable peeler or chocolate curler (available in kitchen specialty stores) to shave the wide side (for wide curls) or thin side (for thin curls) of a chocolate square.

To make long, thin, loosely formed curls, melt 6 chocolate squares and pour into a foil-lined $3^1/_4$ x $5^1/_4$-inch loaf pan. Chill until chocolate is set (about 2 hours). Remove from pan and remove foil. Rub chocolate over shredding side (large holes) of a grater to form curls.

To make large curls, melt about 5 chocolate squares and pour into a jellyroll pan or onto a cookie sheet. Spread chocolate over pan. Chill about 10 minutes. Scrape across surface of chocolate with a long metal spatula, knife, teaspoon, or chocolate curler to form curls. The spatula and knife will form long, thin curls and the teaspoon and curler will form shorter curls. Return pan to refrigerator if chocolate becomes too soft. Use a toothpick to pick up curls.

# metric equivalents

The recipes that appear in this cookbook use the standard United States method for measuring liquid and dry or solid ingredients (teaspoons, tablespoons, and cups). The information on this chart is provided to help cooks outside the U.S. successfully use these recipes. All equivalents are approximate.

## METRIC EQUIVALENTS FOR DIFFERENT TYPES OF INGREDIENTS

A standard cup measure of a dry or solid ingredient will vary in weight depending on the type of ingredient. A standard cup of liquid is the same volume for any type of liquid. Use the following chart when converting standard cup measures to grams (weight) or milliliters (volume).

| Standard Cup | Fine Powder (ex. flour) | Grain (ex. rice) | Granular (ex. sugar) | Liquid Solids (ex. butter) | Liquid (ex. milk) |
|---|---|---|---|---|---|
| 1 | 140 g | 150 g | 190 g | 200 g | 240 ml |
| ¾ | 105 g | 113 g | 143 g | 150 g | 180 ml |
| ⅔ | 93 g | 100 g | 125 g | 133 g | 160 ml |
| ½ | 70 g | 75 g | 95 g | 100 g | 120 ml |
| ⅓ | 47 g | 50 g | 63 g | 67 g | 80 ml |
| ¼ | 35 g | 38 g | 48 g | 50 g | 60 ml |
| ⅛ | 18 g | 19 g | 24 g | 25 g | 30 ml |

## USEFUL EQUIVALENTS FOR LIQUID INGREDIENTS BY VOLUME

| | | | | | | |
|---|---|---|---|---|---|---|
| ¼ tsp | | | | = | 1 ml | |
| ½ tsp | | | | = | 2 ml | |
| 1 tsp | | | | = | 5 ml | |
| 3 tsp | = 1 tbls | | ½ fl oz | = | 15 ml | |
| | 2 tbls | = ⅛ cup | = 1 fl oz | = | 30 ml | |
| | 4 tbls | = ¼ cup | = 2 fl oz | = | 60 ml | |
| | 5 ⅓ tbls | = ⅓ cup | = 3 fl oz | = | 80 ml | |
| | 8 tbls | = ½ cup | = 4 fl oz | = | 120 ml | |
| | 10 ⅔ tbls | = ⅔ cup | = 5 fl oz | = | 160 ml | |
| | 12 tbls | = ¾ cup | = 6 fl oz | = | 180 ml | |
| | 16 tbls | = 1 cup | = 8 fl oz | = | 240 ml | |
| 1 pt | = 2 cups | = 16 fl oz | = | 480 ml | |
| 1 qt | = 4 cups | = 32 fl oz | = | 960 ml | |
| | | | = 33 fl oz | = | 1000 ml | = 1 liter |

## USEFUL EQUIVALENTS FOR DRY INGREDIENTS BY WEIGHT
(To convert ounces to grams, multiply the number of ounces by 30.)

| | | | | | |
|---|---|---|---|---|---|
| 1 oz | = | ¹⁄₁₆ lb | = | 30 g |
| 4 oz | = | ¼ lb | = | 120 g |
| 8 oz | = | ½ lb | = | 240 g |
| 12 oz | = | ¾ lb | = | 360 g |
| 16 oz | = | 1 lb | = | 480 g |

## USEFUL EQUIVALENTS FOR LENGTH

(To convert inches to centimeters, multiply the number of inches by 2.5.)

| | | | | | | | |
|---|---|---|---|---|---|---|---|
| 1 in | | | | | = | 2.5 cm | |
| 6 in | = | ½ ft | | | = | 15 cm | |
| 12 in | = | 1 ft | | | = | 30 cm | |
| 36 in | = | 3 ft | = | 1 yd | = | 90 cm | |
| 40 in | | | | | = | 100 cm | = 1 m |

## USEFUL EQUIVALENTS FOR COOKING/OVEN TEMPERATURES

| | Fahrenheit | Celsius | Gas Mark |
|---|---|---|---|
| Freeze Water | 32° F | 0° C | |
| Room Temperature | 68° F | 20° C | |
| Boil Water | 212° F | 100° C | |
| Bake | 325° F | 160° C | 3 |
| | 350° F | 180° C | 4 |
| | 375° F | 190° C | 5 |
| | 400° F | 200° C | 6 |
| | 425° F | 220° C | 7 |
| | 450° F | 230° C | 8 |
| Broil | | | Grill |

# recipe index